life&debt

a fresh approach to achieving financial wellness

Leslie Tayne, Esq.

GATEWAY BRIDGE

Introduction   *ix*

Part One: What Is Debt?

1 Good Debt vs. Bad Debt   3

2 Different Types of Debt   6

3 Why Debt Must Fit into Your Budget   15

Part Two: The Budget

4 Why Budgeting Is Essential   22

5 How to Create a Budget   27

6 Essential Budget Elements   32

7 Six Common Budgeting Mistakes
       and How to Fix Them   46

8 Six Sample Budgets   51

Part Three: Credit

9 Why Credit Is Important and
       When You Will Need It   68

10 What Affects Your Credit?   72

11 The Next Level of Debt Collection   79

12 What Is Your Credit Report, Your Credit
        Score, and How to Get Copies of Each   85

13 How to Read Your Credit Report   94

14 Myths and Facts About Credit   103

Part Four: The Next Steps

15 The Many Benefits of *Life & Debt*   110

16 Debt Reduction   114

17 Breaking the Credit Card Addiction   120

18 Planning for the Unexpected   125

19 Reducing Debt-Related Stress   130

20 Long-Term Goals   134

21 Leaving the Paycheck-to-Paycheck
        Lifestyle Behind   139

Appendix I: FAQs   141

Appendix II: Sample Credit Report   147

Acknowledgements   153

There was a time when I was drowning in debt. Determined to
free myself from denial and financial turmoil, I sought answers
— and found them. Today I run a successful debt resolution law
practice based on the lessons I learned in my own financial life.
My clients trust me because they know I understand what they
are going through. As a "debt therapist" I provide real-world
solutions to debt-related problems.

Life & Debt: A Fresh Approach to Achieving Financial Wellness
is designed to provide the tools you need to help take charge
of your finances and embrace life with debt. I will show you
how to love having debt. Yes, that's right. Debt is a part of life
and most of us cannot have the things we need, like homes and
cars, without it. Debt is a good and necessary thing — even
Donald Trump has it!

Using a combination of real-world success stories, plus
the detailed application of my debt resolution techniques,
Life &Debt will teach you to put fear and denial aside and set a
new and better course for your life.

My own financial turnaround started by exploring my first
memories of money. I grew up in a well-to-do Long Island,
New York suburb. My parents worked, though my father had
complete control of the family finances. We were far from
destitute yet I remember money was always an issue — and not
a good one. What I learned was money was a dirty word and

something my parents always were arguing about it. Money, therefore, became synonymous with problems.

Since my father controlled the money, and mother never seemed to have any, I made the decision at an early age never to rely on anyone else for money. I was always ambitious and started working in my early teens, first as a babysitter, then in retail stores. I also knew I wanted the independence and respect that comes with a professional career. Law was my childhood dream and I was determined to go to law school. I discovered it was easy to finance my law degree using private and federal student loans. I had no other options. I wanted to be a lawyer and this was a means to an end. I simply signed on the dotted line and did not think about what it would mean to repay those loans. I figured it would all work out later. I was mistaken.

By the time I passed the bar I was married, pregnant with no real job, and $80,000 in student loan debt. Though I had met most of my childhood goals, I was facing one of life's most important lessons — I had accrued debt which needed to be paid back regardless of whether I was paying attention to it or not. My husband worked, and since he took care of the bills, I assumed he was taking care of my loans.

Looking back I see that I repeated the patterns imprinted in childhood by allowing my husband to control the household money. He had a "system" and, with a family that now included three children and a career to juggle, it seemed easier to let him take care of everything. In retrospect, it proved to be a costly mistake.

Unbeknownst to me my student loan repayments went to the bottom of the bill pile. The paperwork was mishandled and eventually the loans went into default. I was sued by my private student loan company and ended up owing twice as much as the original loans. Worse, my credit was destroyed. When I finally faced the situation I was deeply worried. This degree of debt made me feel trapped and embarrassed. I was a lawyer. How could I let this happen?

I immediately took over the management of my loans. The private loans were repaid with family money, but the rest took me years to pay off. I paid them faithfully each month until the day came when I could say goodbye to the loans forever. I will never forget that payment amount — $923.31 per month. The bottom line was I paid twice as much for my legal education.

It took many years, but I worked hard and paid off everything. I learned a great deal and built a successful debt resolution law practice based on what I accomplished in my own life.

Today, I am free from student loan debt because I took control and found real-world solutions to real-world problems — the kind that come across my desk every single day. I teach people from all walks of life, demographics and income brackets how to manage their money, embrace and "love" their debt. With *Life & Debt* you will learn my practical, proven, and easy to-follow techniques. It is a debt therapy session just for you.

The first three sections cover the foundations of finance and how to properly understand debt so you have the tools to manage it. The last section is a way to reap the benefits from your hard work and learn to enjoy your life again without fear of drowning in debt, bills, stress, and the pain that comes with it.

The following are some of the ways I am going to show you how to take charge of your debt:

- How to distinguish between good debt and bad debt
- The different types of debt
- How to manage your debt efficiently and live with it
- Why budgeting is essential, and how to create a realistic budget for any scenario

- Demystifying credit scores, and how to obtain your credit report
- Breaking the credit card addiction
- Planning for the unexpected
- How to leave the paycheck-to-paycheck lifestyle behind

Congratulations. You have already taken the first step. *Life & Debt* will now do the rest.

Part One:

What Is Debt?

CHAPTER **1**

Good Debt vs. Bad Debt

When clients come to me for help one of the first things I do is "demystify" the word debt. With so much financial misinformation in our society many people think of debt as a dirty word, or something to be feared. Both are untrue.

Debt means you owe someone, or something, money. It could be a bank, friend, or family member. Since no one can be debt-free and have a mortgage, car loan, credit card, student loan, or even a bank account, I teach people to embrace their debt and learn to manage it properly so they will love paying their bills at the end of every month instead of dreading them.

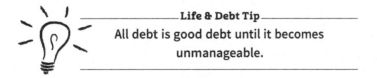

_____Life & Debt Tip_____
All debt is good debt until it becomes
unmanageable.

Good debt is any debt you acquire with the ability to pay back for the term of the loan. Let's say you apply for a car loan. Most people would not seek a car loan knowing they might be out of a job in two months, so you have applied because you have a job and enough income to make the payments.

When your loan is approved that is *good debt* because it means an institution trusted you enough to loan you money for something you need. Debt is only bad when it becomes unmanageable.

What do I mean by unmanageable? To be realistic, all debt comes with strings attached. The question is which strings are thicker than others, and which ones are pulled harder. The answer will tell you whether the debt you have is good or bad.

Example: If you have borrowed $100,000 from your in-laws and are paying it back comfortably with no complaints from them, that is good debt. However, if your in-laws are constantly harassing you and complaining to the point that it is impacting you emotionally and financially, then your good debt has become bad debt.

John and Susan's Story

The recent economic downturn hit all income brackets, which is why John and Susan came to me seeking help. Everything changed for this two-income professional couple who had lived comfortably within their means until John lost his job. With two children and mounting expenses Susan's salary was not enough to cover the bills so they started supplementing expenses with credit cards — always a recipe for financial disaster.

Previously they only used credits cards for unexpected expenses and quickly paid off the balances. Now they could hardly pay the card minimums. When they no longer could make regular mortgage payments they contacted me.

At first they were embarrassed. After assuring them there was no shame in their situation, and they were not unique, we got to work. I made a detailed study of their entire financial situation, listed creditors and minimum payments, reviewed what types of debt they carried — good and bad, set up spread sheets and devised a budget for short-term and long-term financial planning.

Today, John and Susan are once again living comfortably within their means. We resolved the debt that had plagued them, and make sure they stay on track by re-evaluating their budget and finances on a regular basis.

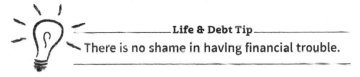

Life & Debt Tip
There is no shame in having financial trouble.

There is no shame in having financial trouble. Many people find themselves in over their heads — and it can happen quickly. Instead of being embarrassed, I tell my clients to be proud of themselves for recognizing they needed help.

By reading this book you have already chosen to demystify your debt and seek help. You now understand the difference between good debt and bad debt. Let's continue and I will show you how to take control of your finances and learn to love paying your bills.

CHAPTER *2*

Different Types of Debt

The more you know about debt, the more it will work for you instead of against you. In this chapter I will show you different types of debt — secured and unsecured — and the responsibilities that come with each. Remember, knowledge is power when it comes to your finances.

SECURED DEBT

Secured debt means that the loan you have taken out is "secured" by a physical item of value. This might be a car, home, boat, or something the creditor could repossess if you default (meaning you did not repay) on your loan. It depends on your credit score but generally interest rates are lower on secured debt because the creditor can claim the secured item, if necessary, to offset the money you owe. In general a secured debt has a written agreement and a security item (instrument).

UNSECURED DEBT

Unsecured debt is not linked to a tangible item. This can encompass everything from personal loans to credit card debt. For example, if you stop paying your credit card bill, there is no piece of property tied to the debt which the creditor can immediately take possession of. This does not mean you get a free pass. There are serious consequences when you don't pay your debts, and the credit card companies are not in the business of forgiveness. You could face late fees, higher interest rates, or even a lawsuit.

HYBRID DEBT

Hybrid loans are a combination of secured and unsecured debt. A hybrid debt could start out unsecured, but then become secured due to circumstances. Let's say you borrow money from a family member. Though you have a strong motivation to pay it back to preserve family harmony, your debt is theoretically unsecured because there is nothing in writing. Unfortunately you lose your job and cannot make the payments. Will that family member accept your troubles with a smile, or seek a judgment against you in the courts and maybe put a lien on your property? If you don't want to get caught on the wrong side of that question, always know your creditor and what your options are before you take on debt.

Life & Debt Tip

Know the creditors' rights on secured and unsecured loans and what you might be legally responsible for if you default.

Now that you know the basics of secured, unsecured, and hybrid debt let's take a look at some of the specific types of debt you are likely to encounter in your lifetime.

STUDENT LOANS

Today's college costs can run anywhere from $15,000 to $35,000 per year for just the basics. It is no surprise that recent reports state the overwhelming majority of college students now receive some type of financial aid. Student loan debt has exceeded $1 trillion dollars in the United States alone. Worse, more than half of that money must be repaid by those students, since the debt is in their names.

Student loans are rarely dischargeable in bankruptcy. Before you take out a student loan read the fine print and make sure you understand the payment terms, which are when you begin payment, how much will you pay, and for how long.

Also be aware of the deferment and forbearance terms, which vary given the type of loan, and the consequences of defaulting (nonpayment). A deferment is when the loan company grants you a break from paying your loan for a fixed amount of time, but you still may be liable for interest charges. A forbearance is when the loan company cannot grant a deferment but will allow you to stop paying the loan or reduce your payments for a period of time but you will still be charged interest.

I had a client who did not receive her degree until 20 years after she graduated. Some universities will allow you to borrow directly from them to supplement any private or government loans. My client took a loan out for $15,000 from the college she was attending and made a verbal agreement to pay down her loan interest free. Unfortunately her loan started accruing interest without her knowledge after the person she made the original agreement with left the University. Imagine my client's surprise when she learned she now owed twice the amount of the original loan! The University held onto her diploma until everything was paid in full. I cannot emphasize enough to always know your responsibilities, understand the terms, and always get it in writing, not just with student loans, but with all loans.

—————— **Life & Debt Tip** ——————
Before you take on any student loans learn
the responsibilities that come with them,
and always retain a written copy of the
original agreement.

BANK CREDIT CARD

The secret to using credit cards without accruing mountains of debt is to just have a few and use them responsibly. There are many different types of credit cards, each with different terms conditions, interest rates, and credit limits. Choosing the right one depends on your personal situation and you should only carry a *manageable* amount of debt on that card. For example, if you have $5,000 in available credit, you should carry no more than $1,500 of debt. If you cannot pay the balance off every month, make sure you pay at least double the minimum payment. The banks will make a lot of money off you if you only pay the minimum amount. You could face decades of payments with a total that is double, or even triple, the original balance.

The Credit Card Accountability, Responsibility, and Disclosure Act (CARD) mandates that every credit card statement explains how long it will take to pay down your debt if you only pay the minimum. Some even have your credit score listed.

Minimum Payment Warning: If you make only the minimum payment each period, you will pay more in interest and it will take you longer to pay off your balance. For example, on a $500 debt with a 15% interest rate:

If you make no additional charges using this card and each month you pay ...	You will pay off the balance shown on this statement in about ...	And you will end up paying an estimated total of ...
Only the minimum payment of $20	3 years	$634.25
$40	2 years	$575.50 (Savings = $58.75)

———————————— **Life & Debt Tip** ————————————

If you cannot pay the full credit card balance off every month, make sure you pay at least double the minimum requirement.

RETAIL STORE CREDIT CARD

Retail stores want your money and they will jump through hoops to get it. How many times have you made a purchase where the salesperson has offered you a discount *on the spot* if you apply for a store credit card? This hard sell, plus future discounts and coupons, are difficult to resist. Be aware that store cards come with different terms and stipulations than regular bank credit cards, such as higher interest rates. I believe store cards are not worth it unless you are disciplined enough to pay the balance at the end of the month. When you are at the register and asked if you want a store credit card, "just say no."

Lisa's Story

When Lisa G. opened her wallet I knew immediately why she fell into deep financial trouble — she had at least 10 store credit cards! She was a victim of the enticing on-the-spot discount for opening an instant credit card. Worse, every time she opened a store account she was bombarded by emails loaded with "special coupons" to be used with her brand new card.

It took some time, however, with the budget I devised for Lisa, she was able to pay off the cards and learn to live within her means. I also taught her my retail store system — one card for one store only. Lisa now takes advantage of the generous discounts at her favorite store but only buys an item she has budgeted for in advance. She does not carry a balance on that card, and uses a general credit card or a debit card for other purchases.

RETIREMENT DEBT

In general, retirement debt is a loan you borrow from your retirement savings or similar tax-deferred savings. It is not a good idea to take a loan from either because you are borrowing against your future. True, it is your money, but you usually have less time to pay it back than a traditional personal loan or other form of unsecured debt. On top of the interest charged there are serious tax penalties if you are unable to pay it back on time. You could be liable for a 10% early withdrawal penalty on the full amount borrowed, and be taxed on whatever portion you do not repay. Also, your employer may not allow you to make your regular pretax contributions during the repayment period, resulting in less retirement money being saved.

Bill's Story

Bill M. is a civil servant who makes a good salary and has saved money in a 401(k). Unfortunately he made the mistake of treating his retirement account like an ATM machine.

Bill took a personal loan at 7% interest from his 401(k) to pay off $25,000 in credit card debt. "It was so easy. In five minutes I had my loan," said Bill. You might wonder why this was a bad financial decision. Yes, he paid off his cards, but he only substituted one loan for another without addressing the underlying issue — *cash flow*. Despite earning a good living, Bill did not know how to budget, and because of that, he could not live within his means no matter how many loans he took out.

After taking the loan on his 401(k) he had less take-home pay because it was deducted directly from his salary, less retirement money and more credit card troubles. Why? He did not know how to manage his cash flow. In my experience nine out of 10 people like Bill end up racking up large credit card debts again — which is exactly where he was when he came to me. I immediately put him on a budget and he is slowly paying off his debts and replenishing his retirement savings.

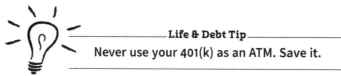

Life & Debt Tip

Never use your 401(k) as an ATM. Save it.

Other Debt Scenarios

BANK OVERDRAFT

An overdraft on a checking account is a bank loan, plain and simple. If you go into overdraft on your checking account by not having enough money in it to cover the checks you've written, you will most likely be charged a fee. Most likely this won't come as a bill but be deducted from future funds you deposit. It is nearly impossible to know what a current balance is and fees can rack up quickly. It is "a vicious cycle" as one client described. I never choose an overdraft option when I open a new bank account, and I strongly advise you do not either. If you have enough money you will not need it, if you don't have enough money you will only get in deeper debt.

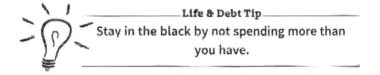

Life & Debt Tip
Stay in the black by not spending more than you have.

MEDICAL EXPENSES DEBT

Medical debt occurs when your insurance company does not pay the full cost of a medical procedure, or you did not have health insurance to start with. Medical costs can be prohibitive, especially if you have a serious illness requiring hospitalization or frequent costly treatments. I also have clients whose co-pays run into the thousands. I suggest having an emergency ("what if") fund to help cover unexpected expenses like these, which we will discuss in more detail later. You may also try calling the hospital or doctor's office to see if you can agree on a payment plan that works with your budget.

HOUSEHOLD DEBT

Believe it or not, cable or electric bills are a form of hybrid debt. Although these companies are not lending you money, you are using their services with the commitment to pay for those services at the end of each month. If you do not pay, then you will lose those services.

Now that we have looked at the many types of debt, it is time to address where your debt should fit into your budget.

CHAPTER *3*

Why Debt Must Fit into Your Budget

The classic American Dream of living "the good life" is something most people aspire to, but it comes with a price tag. Whether it is a home mortgage, car loan or line of credit, debt is the price we pay for our dreams and, if not managed properly, dreams can become financial nightmares.

Step one to managing your debt is understanding how and why it fits into your budget. I will show you how to create and maintain a detailed budget in the next section, but for now let's look at why debt needs a place in your budget.

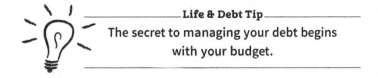

Life & Debt Tip
The secret to managing your debt begins
with your budget.

Budget 101

A budget consists of two equally important components — money coming in (income) and money going out (expenses). Let's start with your income, which is your take-home pay after taxes and other payroll deductions. You might be surprised to learn that, when queried, many of my clients cannot tell me what their take-home (net) pay is. If you are one of these people then start by looking at your pay stub. The larger number is your "gross" pay. The smaller number is your "net" pay. Net pay is the money you take home every pay period after all your deductions are made such as taxes, social security, 401(k) and insurance.

Charles' Story

If your income varies from month to month you must use a lower earning month to calculate your budget, not a higher one. My client Charles H. takes home $4,000 per month but sometimes his overtime nets him $5,000-plus per month. To do a monthly budget, he needs to calculate his income based on the $4,000 figure, not $5,000. The former is a fixed number and the latter is variable. Unfortunately he made a common mistake and was budgeting based on the higher number, which put him deeply in debt.

Once Charles' net income was determined we listed all his bills, which made up the expense portion of his budget. To do this I suggested he start with the first day of the month and write down everything he spends. I will describe this method in greater detail in the next section, but expenditures include mortgage, car payment, student loan payments, credit card payments, utility bills, cable and other expenses. Once I had both sets of figures — money in and money out — I devised a budget that turned his bad debt into good debt.

FINDING BALANCE

The key to turning bad debt into good debt is finding the proper balance in your budget. Most people know that if their monthly income is $5,000 and bills total $7,000 they are in trouble, but few know they are also in trouble if their mortgage is $3,000 with a $5,000 a month income. Why? To stay on a healthy financial path, and avoid bad debt, I suggest your mortgage payment should be no more than one-third of your net pay. Many expenses come with home ownership such as homeowners insurance and taxes, which are variable, meaning the amounts can change. You need to be prepared for the added costs of home ownership. I tell my clients that, ideally, I would like them to budget their housing expenses as one-third of their net pay.

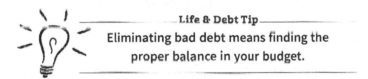

Life & Debt Tip
Eliminating bad debt means finding the
proper balance in your budget.

Bad Debt Leads to More Bad Debt

Jenny's Story

Skating on the edge of bad debt affects you in many unexpected ways, as my client Jenny L. discovered. She came to me for help with mounting credit card debt and the desire to buy a new car. Her current car had logged more than 200,000 miles, and it was clearly time for something new.

Unfortunately, Jenny had 30 credit cards. No joke. She was a classic victim of the relentless "easy credit" marketing machine. "I get a discount when I buy something" she told me. I replied "This is true. But if the discount is 10-20% off and you do not pay the bill in full and accrue a balance with an interest rate of 28%, you are paying more for that item not less."

I also told her that owning 30 credits cards would negatively affect her credit score which would then negatively impact her ability to buy the car she needed. With a bad credit score, or risky credit structure, she was facing higher interest rates, the possibility of a higher down payment, or the need for someone to co-sign (guarantee) the loan.

I taught her how to create an overall budget, which included paying down those credit cards and getting rid of most of them. Then, I did a specific budget for her new car. Soon Jenny was turning bad debt into good debt, and reaping the benefits. By eliminating her morning specialty coffees, plus her take-out Chinese lunches, she was able to save $60 a week, which totaled $240 per month! That became her new car payment.

BUDGETING FOR THE FUTURE

Budgets come in all shapes and sizes just like debt. We all have life goals, both short-term and long-term, and more often than not they involve debt. Whether you are budgeting for a new car like Jenny L., planning a wedding, looking at graduate schools, deciding on lakefront property, or setting a travel itinerary for when you retire, you need to plan ahead financially to make it happen. That means your goals and finances must run on parallel tracks and be revisited regularly to make sure they stay on course and not crash.

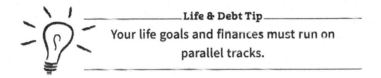

————————Life & Debt Tip————————
Your life goals and finances must run on
parallel tracks.

Plan to re-evaluate your goals and budgets frequently because life can change very quickly. I have clients tell me they don't care about their credit scores. Often they are married or think they have a secure safety net — but what happens if they get divorced or their income drops? You must rely on yourself when dealing with your credit score — be aware of it and what it will do for you. I will show you how to do that later, but, for now, know that your credit score is your passport to the things you need in life.

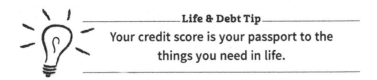

————————Life & Debt Tip————————
Your credit score is your passport to the
things you need in life.

Future goals can vary depending on your age, socio-economic status, employment, and finances. They all start with a detailed budget. Each debt has a time frame even if some, like mortgages, seem to go on forever. When properly managed, your debts will be repaid as your life goals are met. Now let's get started on your budget.

Future Goals

What is your future goal? It can be anything! Here are some examples:

- Marriage
- Buy a home
- Have kids
- Buy a second home
- Buy a boat
- Go on vacation
- Be ready for retirement
- Pay for your child's college education (or grandchild's)
- Pay off credit card debt
- Change careers
- Go back to college and pay your way
- Buy a new car
- Retire early
- Pay off student loans

Part Two:

The Budget

CHAPTER

Why Budgeting Is Essential

The single most important tool for resolving bad debt and avoiding its consequences is learning how to budget. It is essential to balance what you are earning with what you are spending, and the only way to do that effectively, for the majority of people, is to budget.

In this section I will show you my easy and "pain-free" way to achieve the financial stability you deserve. But first, let's dispel some myths which surround the word "budget."

ANTI-BUDGETERS

About 80% of the clients who come to me for help have never budgeted. They run the gamut from those who are unsure of how to get started, to serious avoiders, which I call "the anti-budgeters." The latter steadfastly refuse to consider budgeting and have not made the connection that if they did, they would not be in my office. First I assure all my clients they made the right decision in seeking help, and then I show them how to put their financial life back on a healthy track.

William's Story

My client William C. is a smart man. He earns a good living, has a lovely home and family, and a lifestyle that typifies the American Dream. He has one problem, however, which jeopardizes all of it — he is deeply in debt and refuses to budget. "It's not my style," he told me. Then he asked, "I make a good living, so why am I in debt?" William is a classic anti-budgeter. He does not equate the necessity of budgeting to solving his problem. He thinks it is something done in the office, not in the home.

First I had to convince William that without a budget his bad debt could not be resolved. Second, I had to show him how easy and painless it can be. I will talk more about that in later chapters. William's resistance is common and often based on fear — and no one likes to admit they are afraid.

How to Confront the Fear of Budgeting

Let's talk start with these two questions:

- How much do you earn every month?
- How much do you spend every month?

If you cannot answer either — or both — then you have an issue with budgeting that might be rooted in a simple fear of the unknown. "To thine own self be true," said William Shakespeare and, recognizing your fear is the first step to conquering it.

I had a client who was so paralyzed with fear due to mounting bills and bad debt that she placed all her bills and back statements *unopened* in a large shopping bag in a corner of her living room. She could not even look at them and was a classic victim of "financial avoidance." She actually thought that she might fall victim to the "bag lady syndrome," which is the fear of being destitute. She brought the shopping bag to our first meeting and it took hours to sort through the contents.

> **NOTE:** This fear is not gender-specific and crosses all socio-economic lines.

No matter how bad things might seem, stay focused. Going into denial will only make matters worse. She accrued exorbitant overdraft fees and nearly ruined her credit score. Today, she is still digging out from under but on the right path with a budget. I also taught her the crucial difference between needs and wants.

Needs vs. Wants

A budget is a list of money coming in and money going out. To create one you need both sets of figures, which I address later in this section. However, to stay on the right path financially you must also learn the difference between needs and wants in your spending habits.

The following is an essential question:

What are you spending your money on?

I ask my clients to make a list of all their monthly expenditures including mortgage, utilities, insurance, health, and household expenses. They are often surprised when we review needs vs.

wants on that list. Surprise can turn to happiness when needs and wants are balanced properly.

Example: An electric bill is a necessity, but 250 extra movie channels are not. I have heard justifications for spending extra money on everything from season tickets and 500-plus HDTV channels to daily specialty coffees (at $5 to $10 per cup) and shopping at expensive boutiques.

All of this is elective spending and there is nothing wrong with it — unless you are deeply in debt and trying to cut costs. I teach my clients how to trim elective spending and still enjoy "the good life" because trimming unnecessary costs gives you more money at the end of the month.

Simple Budget Advice: Grocery Shopping

Today's technology makes everything a little easier and that includes budgeting. Smartphones have calculators and I suggest you use them at the grocery store — or any store for that matter. Never go into a store without a list and a fixed amount of you want to spend. If you have budgeted $100, only spend that amount. How many times have you said, "I went to the store for a carton of milk and spent $50." You would be amazed at how much money you can save with this simple system.

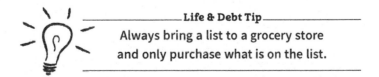

—————————— **Life & Debt Tip** ——————————
Always bring a list to a grocery store
and only purchase what is on the list.

In the next chapter I will show you how to create a budget. Be assured you are in safe hands. I have taught thousands of people that budgeting is nothing to fear. On the contrary, it is easy, fun, and rewarding. Not only will it keep you from being crushed under mountains of bad debt, it will improve your quality of life in many surprising ways.

CHAPTER

How to Create a Budget

Budgets have only one rule — do not spend more than you earn. It may sound simplistic but if you do not go over your budget, you will not accrue bad debt. A budget is not a new idea but it is far simpler to create and follow than most people think. Once you get in the habit of doing one, you enjoy the benefits of controlling your money instead of it controlling you. Let's get started.

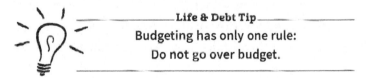

—Life & Debt Tip—
Budgeting has only one rule:
Do not go over budget.

WHAT IS A BUDGET?

A budget lists the money you earn each month and the money you pay out each month — money coming in and money going out. Since 99% of us do both each month, you already have the two essentials for creating a budget — simple, right? Now I will show you how to apply them.

INCOME: MONEY COMING IN

The first step to budgeting is knowing how much net income you earn each month. Net means your "take-home" pay after taxes, social security, insurance, and retirement contributions (where applicable) are deducted from your base salary. Your pay stub will show you the exact amount of net income you have after deductions. If you have additional income sources such as pension checks, dividends or cash *(see pg. 30, "When Your Income Is Cash)*, these need to be added to the list. The total of net income, plus any supplemental income, is the amount of money you actually earn each month.

EXPENDITURES: MONEY GOING OUT

Money going out generally means bills and monthly expenses. I will provide a detailed list in the next chapter but expenses should consist of three separate categories: fixed, variable, and discretionary. Fixed include set amounts per month such as mortgage, car payments, cable, phone, and insurance. Variable expenses can change depending on needs and include food, gas, toiletries, and medications. Discretionary is elective spending — the "lifestyle choices" we enjoy such as eating out and vacations. All three combined total your monthly expenditures. In the next chapter I will show you the pitfalls/rewards of each, and how to balance them.

SAVINGS: A BENEFICIAL EXPENSE

Savings is a sub-category of monthly expenses but an important one. I advocate putting some money into a saving account each month if possible. I do this myself and call it the "10% off the top" expenditure, meaning I move 10% of my net income into my savings account before I pay any other expenses. You are giving the gift of extra money to yourself. It also creates a "what if" fund if needed.

Making It Work Together

Once we make a detailed list of money coming in and money going out we can locate the sources/causes of your bad debt and fix the problems. Though your problems might seem overwhelming now, please be assured they can be fixed. Many of my clients are surprised to discover which areas of their spending put them on the fast track to being in the red.

Mary's Story

It is very easy to overestimate what you make, which is why budgeting is essential. Some people try to keep figures in their heads, but few of us are human calculators as my client Mary C. discovered. She thought she could keep track of her monthly income expenditures without writing them down. This led her to believe she had enough to afford payments on the luxury car of her dreams. She soon found out that she could afford the car payments but little else and ended up living paycheck to paycheck while slowly accruing bad debt by using her credit cards to cover other expenses. However, a few minutes each day, with a budget I devised for her, fixed her problem and she is enjoying her car without financial stress.

TOOLS FOR BUDGETING

This is so easy — all you really need is a pen and paper. A budget is made up of simple lists so, however you make lists these days, be it paper, Smartphone, computer or iPad, you have the basic tools. However, I highly recommend a calculator, which is readily available everywhere.

WHEN TO BUDGET

I like to have a relatively calm and comfortable environment when I do my budgets so a weekend morning before all the activities start usually works best for me. However, you might find it ideal to work on your budget at night, or at the office during your lunch break. The beauty of budgeting is you can choose the time that works best for you.

There are certain times in your life when starting a budget is less advisable. This could be after a large windfall like an inheritance or a large expense such as a wedding. I believe it's best to start when your income and expenses are more stable so you have a better idea of actual numbers.

When Your Income Is Cash

They say cash is king and very often that is true, as long as you follow the rules. If you have a cash business, or supplemental cash income, you must report it to the IRS *and to your budget* — both will keep you out of trouble and in the black. Also, cash is so tempting to spend. A $20 purchase at the grocery store can easily turn into $100. I also know people who take cash out of their businesses to pay bills. It's called a draw. That money is not "free" just because it is their business. It has tax consequences that must be met. The bottom line: be careful with cash.

GETTING STARTED: BOOT CAMP FOR BEGINNERS

There are many ways to create a budget, but getting in the habit of understanding how you are spending your money is key to all — and essential for beginners. There is a simple way to learn what your variable and discretionary expenses are. Keep a small notebook with you, or use your Smartphone or tablet and write down everything you spend (or take a picture) from a morning latte, to groceries and dinner with friends, for one week. Once you see how easy one week is, increase it to two and then finish the month.

After a month you can congratulate yourself on completing the first and most important step to successful budgeting — learning how you spend your money each month. It is a very exciting beginning. In the next chapter I will show you how to use that knowledge to balance your budget.

CHAPTER *6*

Essential Budget Elements

A budget consists of two separate lists — one showing money coming in (income) and the other showing money going out (expenses). Balancing your budget begins with knowing what belongs on each list, which you will learn in this chapter.

Tips Before You Begin

STAY MOTIVATED

Motivation is a key to success. Since you are reading this book, you are already motivated, which is a wonderful way to begin. My system is easy to understand and utilize, but like anything worthwhile, it does require learning some simple steps such as setting goals, creating a guideline for monthly expenses, and finding someone who will support you through the process. That said, stay motivated, take your time, and do not get discouraged. Soon you will be one of the many people who have achieved financial freedom by using my *Life & Debt* system.

SET GOALS

Goals give us something to look forward to, like a vacation or a buying a new home, and most involve money. Give yourself a small financial goal to meet right away. It will act as a short-term reward and encouragement as you begin to meet your long-term goals of financial freedom. How about a new pair of dress shoes or tickets to a show? With my system meeting financial goals is not stressful — it's exciting and fun.

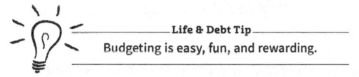
_____Life & Debt Tip_____
Budgeting is easy, fun, and rewarding.

GUIDELINES FOR MONTHLY EXPENSES

Before we discuss budget essentials, here are some general guidelines for your monthly expenses

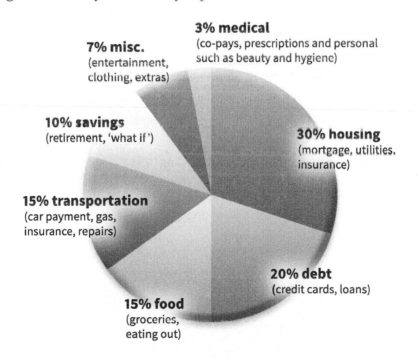

3% medical
(co-pays, prescriptions and personal such as beauty and hygiene)

7% misc.
(entertainment, clothing, extras)

10% savings
(retirement, 'what if')

30% housing
(mortgage, utilities, insurance)

15% transportation
(car payment, gas, insurance, repairs)

20% debt
(credit cards, loans)

15% food
(groceries, eating out)

These percentages will vary depending on your lifestyle choices (discussed later in this chapter), but they are a good starting point. If you are over in one category, like housing for example, there are ways to adjust other categories to compensate. My clients are pleasantly surprised when they see how cutting back and following these guidelines leads to more cash flow and a more comfortable financial future.

Heather and Ken's Sample Budget: Before & After

Their Budget Before Using the *Life & Debt* System

(Based on a monthly net income of $4,000 after taxes and deductions)

Housing (mortgage, utilities, taxes, insurance)	$1,200	(30%)
Food (groceries, eating out)	$1200	(30%)
Transportation (car payment, insurance, gas, maintenance)	$600	(15%)
Medical (prescriptions, doctor's visits, beauty and hygiene supplies)	$120	(3%)
Miscellaneous (entertainment, cell phone, clothing)	$600	(15%)
Savings ("what if" fund, personal savings)	0	
Debt payments (credit cards, loans)	$280	(7%)

Problem: Though transportation and housing were on target, food and miscellaneous were not. As a result, there was no money for savings, emergencies, or paying more toward debt.

Their Budget After Using the *Life & Debt* System

Housing (mortgage, utilities, taxes, insurance)	$1,200	(30%)
Food (groceries, eating out)	$600	(15%)
Transportation (car payment, insurance, gas, maintenance)	$600	(15%)
Medical (prescriptions, doctor's visits, beauty and hygiene supplies)	$120	(3%)
Miscellaneous. (entertainment, cell phone, clothing)	$280	(7%)
Savings ("what if" fund, personal savings)	$400	(10%)
Debt payments (credit cards, loans)	$800	(20%)

Life & Debt Action Taken: I trimmed food expenses by advising them to eat out less and use store coupons. I showed them that expensive entertainment lifestyle choices can be replaced by less pricey or free activities, and switched them to a more affordable cell phone plan.

Result: Heather and Ken have more money for savings and an emergency fund, plus they are paying down their debt.

ESSENTIAL ITEMS: INCOME

This list is very simple. Write down all your monthly income which includes:

- Your "net" employee take-home pay after taxes, social security, deductions
- Supplemental income including cash, eBay, tax refund, work bonus, birthday money

Congratulations you are now halfway through setting up your budget. See how simple that was?

ESSENTIAL ITEMS: EXPENSES

This list has three categories: Fixed, Variable, and Discretionary.

Fixed Expenses

These are bills and expenses which remain fixed (the same amount) every month. They can include:

- Mortgage payments or rent
- Homeowner fees
- Car payments / car insurance
- Cable TV
- Internet
- Health insurance / dental plan
- Utilities if you are on a fixed plan—and you should be
- Dues: gym, associations
- Landline phone
- Loan payments
- Emergency "what if" fund
- Savings

Variable Expenses

These are regular expenses but the amount changes each month:

- Gas and transportation — bus, train, subway
- Car maintenance
- Medical: co-pays, prescriptions, medical equipment
- Credit card payments
- Utilities (if not on a fixed plan)
- Cell phone

- Household maintenance
- Food
- Hygiene/grooming
- Clothing/cleaning
- Pets
- School supplies
- Charities/gifts
- Magazines
- Entertainment
- Legal

Discretionary Expenses: Needs vs. Wants

I call this category "lifestyle choices" and it is different for each person. The best way to address it is to explain needs vs. wants. I once had a client who was $80,000 in debt but believed a $1,000 per-month Mercedes an absolute necessity. A $200 per month car would get him from A to B just as well as a $1,000 per-month car so this was a non-essential expense. The truth is he *wanted* this car, but he certainly didn't *need* it. Because he did not understand the difference between the two he steered right into serious financial trouble. Also with a high-priced luxury car there can be many added expenditures — like gas and insurance.

I am not saying you should deny yourself the good things in life. On the contrary I help people manage their money so they can meet their goals and enjoy their lifestyle choices. However, learning what can be removed from your expenses list, and working within a reasonable budget, gets you the things you want without accruing bad debt and its consequences.

Discretionary expenses has two lists: **Essential** and **Non-essential**. It is my opinion the majority of discretionary spending can be termed non-essential if you are on a budget and motivated to remove bad debt. Take a look at this list and see if anything looks familiar:

- $5 lattes twice a day
- Take out lunches 3-5 days a week
- Designer clothes
- Eating dinner out twice a week
- 400 cable TV stations
- Shopping for non-essentials
- 5-star vacations
- Excessive entertainment
- Season tickets to anything
- Luxury items

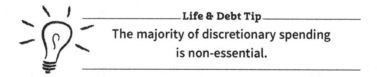

————Life & Debt Tip————
The majority of discretionary spending
is non-essential.

You would be surprised to learn how much money you can save per month by removing just a few of these items. Overspending becomes a habit, but it's one you can break. Learning to live within your budget might seem difficult at first, but think of it as tough love — tough now, but rewarding later.

Margaret's Story

Margaret B. decided to downsize from full-time employment to part-time to spend more time with her first child. Less income is always a challenge, but after a careful review of her discretionary spending, it was clear one of her passions was movies. In some cities today that can be a significant weekly expenditure. One of my solutions was to steer her to the local library where she could borrow free DVDs.

> **NOTE:** Libraries are a wonderful free entertainment resource.

Some of the things you feel you *must* have, you really can do without during the budgeting process. Address them again later when your finances are on the right track.

HIDDEN EXPENSES

No matter how skilled you are at budgeting, life is full of "hidden" expenses — like bringing your car in for an oil change and being told you need a new transmission. Using a credit card to pay for them only leads to more bad debt. The best way to deal with hidden costs is to be prepared. That is why a "what if" fund is listed under my essentials category and should be part of the 10% you are putting into savings each month. Having three-to-nine months' worth of expenses saved for an emergency is ideal, but anything you put aside on a monthly basis will help you with hidden expenses.

STAYING THE COURSE

All new programs have a learning curve and budgeting is no different. Start slow if you like and just organize a few bills into categories. Above all, know there no shame in falling off the budget wagon as long as you come back soon.

Budget Jewel is my proprietary online budget planning system which was designed by my team of credit and debt experts. It offers in-depth analysis and easy-to-follow tools for clients who need solutions to their financial problems. As a special bonus to readers of this book, I can offer you free access at **www.budgetjewel.com** using the code **lifeanddebt15**.

Budget Jewel

WHAT IS BUDGET JEWEL?

Budget Jewel is an easy-to-follow program which makes budgeting simple and effective. Because no account numbers are inputted, it is completely safe and takes the "scare factor" out of using online tools. Until now, Budget Jewel was an online program I provided for my clients to become more comfortable with budgeting.

Simply put, Budget Jewel is a user-friendly way to calculate your monthly budget, or a specific budget, for one-time purchases. Few people who come to my office tell me they like to budget, and since I know how easy Budget Jewel makes this process, I advise them that their perception can change with the right tools. Budget Jewel does not require any special computer skills or knowledge of financial programs. All you need to do is be willing to take the first step.

I called it Budget Jewel because, like a precious stone, it is valuable and can become a great asset to you for years to come. By starting simply you will learn how your income, expenses and the money you spend on bills impact each other. You will also understand what you can and cannot afford by comparing your income to your expenses. This often leads to pleasant surprises. Whether on paper, or on the desktop, there is no better way to learn about your personal finances than through budgeting, and Budget Jewel does the work for you.

It is my belief that budgeting should be easy and a "no brainer," especially for budget beginners who may find many financial programs too complicated. The main reason I created Budget Jewel was to provide an easy point of entry for budget beginners who want to get a grip on their finances. Let Budget Jewel take a snap shot of your finances today and learn how easy and effective budgeting really is.

Vincent's Story

I had a client who was so budget-phobic he even refused to access the calculator on his smart phone to make purchases requiring simple math. As a result, he did not know what he could afford with his income because he did not know what his expenses added up to each month. When he discovered he could not go on the trip of a lifetime with his golfing buddies because his credit cards were maxed out, and he had little money in the bank, he came to me for help.

Once we reviewed his bills he was surprised at

how much he was overspending, and the amount he owed to various creditors. We used www. budgetjewel.com to make the process of taking control of his finances understandable. Afterwards we corrected enough of his existing budgeting mistakes to set him on the right path as a budget-friendly — not budget-phobic person. Because he wanted that golf trip so badly, he made Budget Jewel work for him.

A year later he was able to afford his trip because he budgeted for it while paying down his credit card debt and starting a savings account. He finally knew exactly what he owed his creditors and could always double check any information. It was a new awakening that gave him more financial freedom and relief from debt-related stress.

HOW DOES BUDGET JEWEL WORK?

Budget Jewel is similar to the sample budgets we will review in Chapter 8 where your estimated and actual expenses are listed to calculate an accurate budget. It is important to understand the difference between estimated expenses and actual expenses.

Very often people think they have more money than they do because they have no idea what they spend each month. It is likely they also have no idea who their creditors are and what they owe them. This is an easy trap to fall into for those who do not budget. Also, if your monthly income varies, especially if you do some part-time work for cash or tips, this can be even harder to manage.

The bottom line is if you do not budget all of your expenses and income, and keep track of them, you could accrue more debt and end up in the red every month without knowing it.

Seeing both sets of expenses and income figures helps correct any mistakes in your budget. Staying in the dark about your finances may seem more comfortable then facing reality, but it really isn't.

As I have said, making friends with your budget is a very positive step. It can bring your finances up to the next level and give you the extra things you want in life, like a nice vacation or a second home. It may take a little time and extra effort in the beginning to track your expenses while keeping accurate lists, but it is an important step toward leaving the paycheck-to-paycheck lifestyle behind.

Even people who cannot stand the idea of doing math can use Budget Jewel because the program does the math for you. All you need to get started is to turn on your computer, go to www.budgetjewel.com, create a user name and password and when asked for payment enter: **lifeanddebt15**. You are now good to go. Be positive, keep an open mind and remember you can do this!

Budget Jewel Facts at a Glance

- Created by Leslie Tayne to make budgeting easy and effective
- Free to readers of *Life & Debt*
- Anyone with basic computer skills can use this program
- No math skills required
- Safe and secure online program

Budget Jewel comes with detailed online instructions, but the following screen shot shows you the basics.

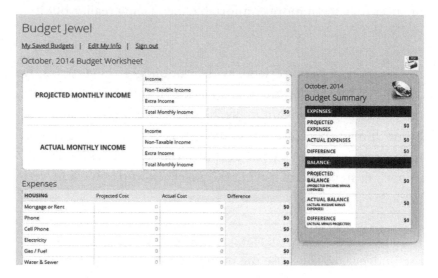

Work from the top down and you only have to fill in the white boxes. After adding all your figures to each section — income and expenses — Budget Jewel will do the rest. You will receive a Budget Summary that is an accurate depiction of your expenses and your remaining balance at the end of the month. Congratulations. You are now on your way.

IS BUDGET JEWEL SAFE TO USE?

Budget Jewel is a safe and secure program. With continuing fears about identity theft (pg. 100) it is important to know that your online financial activity is not being watched, or stolen. Budget Jewel does not operate on a public server and no information is saved or shared with any third parties. Also, you are not imputing any credit card or bank account numbers, simply dollars and cents.

Because I have been offering Budget Jewel to clients for years, it has been very rewarding to see how many have embraced it — and most tell me how easy it is. I remind them it is like a special jewel in their financial toolbox which they should embrace and enjoy because it takes the worry and stress out of budgeting. Budgeting lets you know the two essentials of money management — how much money is coming in (income) and how much money is going out (expenses).

Budget Jewel is a simple and easy way to stay on top of those essentials and leave the paycheck-to-paycheck lifestyle behind.

CHAPTER *7*

Six Common Budgeting Mistakes and How to Fix Them

Nearly everything worthwhile comes with a learning curve and budgeting is no exception. Because I have been doing this for more than 15 years, I am familiar with common budgeting mistakes and how to fix them. Let's take a look at six classic examples.

BUDGET MISTAKE #1: Not Making Friends with Your Budget
Don't laugh but I have known people who would rather have root canal than work on a budget. For them a budget is the enemy. My first step is teaching these clients to wave the white flag.

Life & Debt Fix: A budget is your ticket to getting out of debt, saving money, and achieving your financial dreams. In short, it is the best financial friend you can have. For those who are hesitant to make the leap from foe to friend, I suggest naming your new budget. Call it Candy for something sweet you'd like to buy, or Donald because you want to emulate Donald Trump.

Whether it's Yoda, Toto, Midas, or Mary, the minute you give your new budget a name it stops being an enemy and starts being your friend.

BUDGET MISTAKE #2: Omitting One-Time Annual Expenses
Keeping track of regular monthly expenses like mortgage and utilities is easy because you pay these every month. However, your once-a-year or semi-annual expenses like taxes and insurance premiums have to be part of your budget as well.

Life & Debt Fix: When you first start budgeting, make a new budget for each month and mark on your calendar which months you pay your annual or semi-annual expenses. This also includes magazine subscriptions, dues, and membership fees. After you get the hang of it, make a new budget every six months, or when something significant changes in your financial situation.

BUDGET MISTAKE #3: Not Preparing for the Unexpected
No matter how prepared, our lives can take unexpected turns. Medical bills, home repairs, and emergencies can happen without warning. If you do not have the money to cover these unexpected expenses you can land deeply in debt.

Life & Debt Fix: Add a line item to the expenses portion of your budget called "what if" fund. Treat it just like your mortgage and make regular payments. This fund can rescue you when trouble occurs, or act as a welcome source of cash when you need to buy birthday gifts or school supplies. Having the fund available will give you an extra layer of security and act as an incentive to continue budgeting. Make sure you continue to pay yourself and replenish it.

BUDGET MISTAKE #4: No Savings Account

A savings account is similar to a "what if" fund. Many people consider both elective, but I always counsel that it is essential to your financial and emotional well-being to have some savings — and it's easier than you think.

Life & Debt Fix: Decide on a small amount of money you can reasonably afford to put aside each week. When people tell me they have nothing extra for savings I ask them to try my "$5-a-week latte plan." I think everyone can afford to put $5 a week (the cost of one latte) in a savings account. At the end of one year you will have $260. That is a substantial savings. Give up two lattes a week and it becomes $520. See how you can save money you thought you didn't have?

BUDGET MISTAKE #5: Omitting the Small (Cash) Items

They say the devil is in the details and that is true with budgets. Many people do not keep track of their small cash expenses that really can add up during the course of a month.

Life & Debt Fix: Pay yourself x-amount of cash each week and keep an account of your cash expenses like coffee, dry cleaning, subway fare, taxi, flowers for Mom, lunches, etc. Stay within the amount you have allotted each week and you will stay on budget instead of busting it.

> **NOTE:** Track all your expenditures on a weekly basis instead of waiting until the end of the month.

BUDGET MISTAKE #6: Not Setting Realistic Goals

Starting a budget means you have taken the first step to financial freedom and you are to be congratulated. However, setting unrealistic goals can complicate your budget, lead to confusion, and create a fast track to discouragement — and we don't want that.

Life & Debt Fix: Start slow. Rome wasn't built in a day, and you need time to adjust to keeping track of money going in and money going out. Don't get bogged down in elaborate systems or spreadsheets. Take a look at some of the sample budgets in the next chapter or visit www.budgetjewel.com.

SET A BUDGET DATE: FEEL THE LOVE

Once you start budgeting and see how easy it is to turn your bad debt into good debt (and reap the financial rewards that come with it) you will wonder why you ever thought it was an impossible task. Remember your budget is your friend — set a date with it regularly.

Clara's Story

One of my clients, Clara W., recently had gone through a divorce. During her lengthy marriage her husband handled the finances, paid the bills, and rarely spoke about money. Though she knew very little about the household finances, she was comfortable with the arrangement. She did not have to write a budget, balance a checkbook, or pay a bill. Clara's rude awakening came with the divorce. She wanted to maintain her lifestyle, which included staying in the marital home and driving her pricy SUV with a hefty monthly payment. However her alimony check would not fully support her lifestyle and came with an expiration date. She had to work to supplement her income, which was good, but then started charging most of her expenses to credit cards, which was a bad decision. Up to her eyeballs in debt and deeply worried about her finances, Clara came to me for help.

We quickly devised a "post-divorce" budget that made sense for her income and expenses. I taught her the basics of the *Life & Debt* system so she learned to budget and knew what her income and expenses were each month. We discussed decreasing her car payments and selling the house and buying something smaller and more manageable. I also helped her realize how important it is to put money into a saving account. Though she had a tough learning curve, Clara now is empowered because she is in charge of her finances and her future.

CHAPTER **8**

Six Sample Budgets

Budgets come in all shapes and sizes, from holiday gift lists to purchasing a new home. What they have in common is the ability to achieve your goals without compromising your financial security.

Very often people seek my help because they are deeply in debt, so I make sure I solve their urgent budgeting problems first. However the *Life & Debt* system has a budget solution for all your fiscal considerations including personal financial lifestyle choices.

In this chapter we will look at some sample budgets for Holiday Gifts, Monthly College Expenses, Buying a House, Retirement, Your First Year Pet Care Expenses, and a Standard Monthly Budget. Some are long-term financial commitments, while others are based on a single, one-time expense. Since the Standard Monthly Budget is the largest, and the most comprehensive, I have placed it at the end of the chapter.

> **NOTE:** All of these *Life & Debt* budgets are guidelines only. They are examples for you to review under the suggested circumstances. They are not set in stone because we all have different financial considerations.

Many people are intimidated by math and rightly so. The best part about my *Life & Debt* system is you do not have to be a math whiz or super-organized. I certainly wasn't a math genius back in high school, but I learned the basics first and that is all you need to do. If you use my system for your budget needs, and make a commitment to follow its guidelines, it will work for you.

Start by trying my online budget calculator, Budget Jewel, found at www.budgetjewel.com. Simply insert your income and expenses and, presto, your math anxieties will disappear!

EVERYDAY BUDGET TERMS YOU SHOULD BE FAMILIAR WITH

Before we begin, I suggest getting comfortable with the following terms and their explanations:

Income. For our purposes "income" means your net take-home pay which is *after* taxes and all deductions are taken out of your earned income.

Fixed Income. This income is set at a particular figure each month and does not vary. Examples include social security or pension checks.

Estimated Cost of Item. What you anticipate something will cost.

Actual Cost of Item. What you actually paid, including any taxes, insurance, and shipping costs.

Difference. This tells you if you went over or under your estimated cost for that item.

Total Expenses. The total amount of money used (spent) in a budget.

Total Net. How much money you have remaining after all expenses listed in your budget are deducted from your income.

Holiday Budget for Reggie

His budget: $500

The holidays are a very hectic time of year and whether your gift-giving style is Scrooge or St. Nick, you need a budget plan to help keep the season merry and bright. Starting early on a holiday budget, or any budget, is important and I generally begin my holiday budget in April. Starting early also lets you keep an eye on sales to save money.

First decide how much you can reasonably afford to spend — which means how much can you budget for. Next, make a list of recipients (and decide if you really need a gift for your cousin Steve whom you haven't seen in 20 years). Though holiday spending often feels like it is essential, it is a lifestyle choice. You are in control of how much you spend.

If money is tight, or you just can't give to everyone this year, then consider asking friends and family if they might be interested in putting a cap on gift spending. It might seem like an uncomfortable suggestion, but you'd be surprised how many will say yes *if* you make it fun. For example one of my clients, Jeanne, suggested this to five friends, who loved the idea because they all agreed on a $10 limit. This means the gift was a novelty item and carefully chosen as something small and amusing. Instead of $250 for five gifts that Jeanne could not afford that year, her total was $50 — and all her participants agreed to make it a standard holiday practice. Let's take a look at Reggie D's holiday budget. He gave himself $500 to spend.

Gift Recipient	Gift	Estimated Cost	Actual Cost	Total Cost
Frankie	Beard trimmer	$65	$62.99	$62.99
Robin	Makeup set	$30	$22.60	$85.59
Mike	Cuff links	$50	$68.15	$153.74
Ashley	Doll dream house	$50	$43.60	$197.34
Nancy	Baby doll	$25	$27.30	$224.64
Mark	Football jersey	$90	$110.02	$334.66
Cindy	Bike	$100	$99.80	$434.46
Becky	Scarf and glove set	$20	$15.99	$450.45
Mary	Sweater	$20	$32.68	$483.13
Phil	Wallet	$40	$28.50	$511.63
Luke	Toy truck	$10	$15.82	$527.45
TOTAL		**$500**		**$527.45**

Result: $27.45 over budget

Reggie D. gave himself of budget of $500 and though he was only over by $27.50, to stay within his budget he could have cut one gift or spent a smaller amount on another.

—————————Life & Debt Tip—————————
To help with holiday spending start your shopping early and watch for sales. Also, suggest a spending limit to family and friends.

Monthly Budget for College Student Alex

It is never too early to learn good financial habits, and for many college students, particularly those with student loans, it is imperative they learn to budget. A simple budget showing money coming in and money coming out will give students the parameters for while spending, trying not to accrue more debt. Alex Z. lives off campus and works part-time as a waitress. She is a third-year student and shares a house with several roommates, which cuts her housing costs. Even though her income is variable she was able to stay within her budget and have enough left for a "what if" fund.

Income	Estimated	Actual	Difference
Grants	$100	$100	$0
Scholarships	$900	$900	$0
Loans	$845	$845	$0
Job	$900	$725	–$175
Parents' contribution	$100	$75	–$25
Other income (gifts)	$0	$75	+$75
TOTAL INCOME	**$2,845**	**$2,720**	**–$125**

Academic Expenses	Estimated	Actual	Difference
Tuition and fees	$600	$615	–$15
Books and supplies	$100	$120	–$20
Club/sports fees	$75	$50	+$25

Living Expenses	Estimated	Actual	Difference
Rent	$500	$500	$0
Utilities (water/electric/heat/AC)	$110	$122	–$12
TV/Internet	$90	$98	–$8

continued

Cell phone	$75	$85	–$10
Food	$250	$220	+$30
Credit card payments	$0	$0	$0
Transportation (public/gas)	$50	$75	–$25
Trips home	$80	$0	+$80
Other	$0	$0	$0

Personal Expenses	Estimated	Actual	Difference
Personal (toiletries/hair care/etc.)	$100	$115	–$15
Entertainment	$50	$125	–$75
Clothing/shoes	$0	$60	–$60
Other	$0	$50	–$50
Total Expenses	**$2,080**	**$2,235**	**$155**
TOTAL NET (Income minus Expenses)			**$485**

Alex did well, especially for a college student, and stayed within her budget. It is my suggestion that she apply any extra money toward paying down her student loans. The interest on those loans will keep accumulating as the balance owed grows bigger and bigger. In the end, she could end up with a serious debt to repay after finishing school which is a difficult way to get started.

Life & Debt Tip

College students with extra money at the end of the month should apply it toward paying down their student loans. Graduating with less debt makes the next phase of their lives easier.

Lori and Larry's New Home Budget

Purchasing a home is one of the largest financial investments you will make in your lifetime. It is best to start a budget plan at least two years prior to your purchase so you can save enough money for two reasons. One: you want your down payment be as large as possible so your mortgage will be affordable. Two: there must be enough money left in your accounts after the down payment to show you can afford the mortgage. The amount required will vary but generally you should count on between two and six months of mortgage payments before you close on your house.

With those figures in mind you must decide what you can afford. Housing budgets are complicated and expenses can change. With the *Life & Debt* system we suggest that total housing costs (mortgage, taxes, insurance, utilities, and maintenance fees) should be no more than 30% of your net monthly income.

INCOME & SAVINGS	Amount
Annual income	$70,000
Current savings	$30,000
Annual savings	$5,000

Purchase Details	Amount
Planned monthly housing expenses	$2,100
Home purchase price	$200,000
Maximum mortgage (30 year @ 5%)	$180,000
Down payment needed	$20,000 (~10%)

continued

PMI	$2,740 (one time)
Monthly payments:	
Property taxes	$416.67 ($5,000 a year)
Homeowners insurance	$220
Mortgage payment	$1,073.64
Total monthly payments (including insurance and taxes)	$1,710.31

> **NOTE:** You can choose to do a PMI (private mortgage insurance) as a one-time payment or as monthly payments rolled into your mortgage payment. Know that you will have to pay added interest if you pay monthly.

As I advised, Lori and Larry budgeted two years prior to their purchase. They were able to put down $20,000 on a $200,000 home, had six months of mortgage payments left in their savings account, which they replenish annually and are within the 30% total housing cost budget.

──────────── **Life & Debt Tip** ────────────
When taking out a mortgage consider a longer term, even if the rate is slightly higher. If you make only one extra payment per year to your mortgage principal on a 30 year loan, you could reduce the loan by 10 years. Don't bite off more than you can chew.

Lucy and Ralph's Monthly Retirement Budget

Retirement is a whole new way of life for most people who will now be living on a fixed income. Planning ahead and having savings available to supplement your social security payments is critical. Considering part-time work can be both rewarding and will also help the financial bottom line.

Healthcare costs can skyrocket and if you have Medicare, that means you will not be paying exorbitant monthly health care bills *but* it may only cover about 80% of your medical expenses. Supplemental insurance is something many retirees add to their monthly budget. Also consider paying off your car loan prior to retiring, which will eliminate a large monthly expense. There is always the unexpected at any age, so savings and a "what if" fund are important.

Income	Estimated	Actual	Difference
Retirement savings	$1,000	$1,000	$0
Social Security	$1,100	$1,100	$0
Job	$500	$425	–$75
Other income	$0	$0	$0
TOTAL INCOME	**$2,600**	**$2,525**	**–$75**

Living Expenses	Estimated	Actual	Difference
Rent / mortgage payment	$720	$720	+$0
Utilities (water/electric/heat/AC)	$110	$102	+$8
Landscaping/maintenance	$75	$75	$0
TV/Internet	$90	$98	–$0
Cell phone	$120	$120	$0
Food	$225	$200	+$25
Car payments	$259	$259	$0
Credit card payments	$400	$400	$0
Transportation (public/gas)	$50	$45	+$5
Medical expenses	$125	$100	+$25
Insurance payments	$100	$100	$0
Copays	$75	$25	+$50
Personal (toiletries/hair care/etc.)	$75	$75	$0
Entertainment	$50	$25	+$25
Clothing/shoes	$0	$60	–$60
Savings	$50	$100	–$50
Other	$0	$0	$0
Total Expenses	**$2,524**	**$2,504**	**+$20**
TOTAL NET (Income minus Expenses)			**$21**

Lucy and Ralph's budget shows they planned well. They have a little extra at the end of each month to either add to their savings, or enjoy a special evening out at a favorite restaurant.

_____Life & Debt Tip_____

To know how much money you will need to live comfortably in retirement start your budget, and research where you want to live, at least two years prior.

Jack's First-Year Pet Budget

Today many people consider their pets a member of the family and having a pet includes insuring proper care. Whether you already have pets, are considering adopting your first, or adding to the family, make sure you look carefully at the additional expenses. Some of my clients have accrued large amounts of credit card debt based on veterinary bills. This can be avoided with good planning and a *Life & Debt* budget. When my client Jack decided to adopt a puppy from a shelter I set up this first-year budget for him.

Item	Estimated Cost	Actual Cost	Difference
Adoption fee	$200	$100	+$100
Vet care	$100	$110	−$10
Neuter	$200	$125	+$75
Pet supplies	$50	$90	−$40
Food	$50	$40	+$10
Training	$0	$150	−$150
Home prep	$20	$75	−$55
Grooming	$30	$20	+$10
TOTAL	**$650**	**$710**	**−$60**

Do not be discouraged about adopting a pet based on this first-year budget. Your first-year costs are always the highest due to neutering, spaying, and essential vaccinations. Jack's difference was only $60 and neutering (essential for the health and welfare of your pet) is a one-time expense. Adopting from a shelter can often be less expensive because many shelters will include spay/neutering and micro-chipping with the adoption. Micro-chipping is a tiny chip painlessly implanted in the pet with owner contact information in case you and your pet become separated. Many lost pets are reunited with their owners because of this technology.

Also, older pets require less initial costs and, in general, are already accustomed to living in a home. For dogs that means no "housebreaking" and for cats that means the rambunctious kitten phase is replaced with a calmer companion.

Life & Debt Tip

When thinking about adopting a pet, consider an animal shelter. Often the shelter will spay or neuter for free. Also, older dogs will already be housebroken and older cats calmer. Research pet care health insurance.

A Standard Budget

This is an example of a standard monthly budget. Use it strictly as a guideline since you will want to tailor it to your specific needs and lifestyle. Remember, everyone's financial picture is different!

INCOME
Projected Monthly Income

Income	Non-Taxable Income	Extra Income	Total Monthly Income
$4,200	$0	$0	$4,200

Actual Monthly Income

Income	Non-Taxable Income	Extra Income	Total Monthly Income
$4,200	$50	$0	$4,250

EXPENSES
Housing

Expense	Projected Cost	Actual Cost	Difference
Mortgage or rent	$700	$700	$0
Phone	$30	$30	$0
Cell phone	$75	$80	–$5
Electricity	$45	$48	–$3
Gas/fuel	$250	$225	+$25
Water/sewer	$25	$25	$0
Cable	$75	$75	$0
Waste removal	$15	$15	$0
Maintenance/repairs	$0	$40	–$40
Supplies	$75	$65	+$10
Other	$0	$0	$0
	$1,290	**$1,303**	**–$13**

Transportation

Expense	Projected Cost	Actual Cost	Difference
Vehicle payment	$300	$300	$0
Bus/taxi/train fare	$0	$0	$0
Insurance	$200	$200	$0
Licensing	$0	$0	$0
Fuel	$200	$230	-$30
Maintenance	$0	$35	-$35
Other	$0	$0	$0
$700	**$765**	**-$65**

Insurance

Expense	Projected Cost	Actual Cost	Difference
Home	$150	$150	$0
Health	$100	$100	$0
Life	$100	$100	$0
Other	$0	$0	$0
$350	**$350**	**$0**

Food

Expense	Projected Cost	Actual Cost	Difference
Groceries	$250	$275	-$25
Dining out	$150	$130	+$20
Other	$0	$0	$0
$400	**$405**	**-$5**

Pets

Expense	Projected Cost	Actual Cost	Difference
Food	$50	$50	$0
Medical	$0	$40	-$40
Grooming	$30	$15	+$15
Toys	$10	$0	+$10
Other	$0	$0	$0
$90	**$55**	**-$15**

Personal Care

Expense	Projected Cost	Actual Cost	Difference
Medical	$0	$35	-$35
Hair/nails	$60	$40	+$20
Clothing	$150	$120	+$30
Dry cleaning	$40	$40	$0
Health club	$15	$15	$0
Organization dues or fees	$0	$0	$0
Other	$0	$0	$0
$265	**$250**	**+$15**

Work Expenses

Expense	Projected Cost	Actual Cost	Difference
Breakfast/coffee	$60	$50	+$10
Lunch	$100	$100	$0
Tolls	$10	$10	$0
Supplies	$0	$20	–$20
Other	$0	$0	$0
Other	$0	$0	$0
	$170	**$180**	**–$10**

Entertainment

Expense	Projected Cost	Actual Cost	Difference
Video/DVD	$10	$5	+$5
CDs/MP3s	$0	$0	$0
Movies	$50	$50	$0
Concerts	$0	$60	–$60
Sporting events	$120	$120	$0
Live theatre	$0	$45	–$45
Other	$0	$0	$0
Other	$0	$0	$0
Other	$0	$0	$0
	$180	**$280**	**–$100**

Loans

Expense	Projected Cost	Actual Cost	Difference
Personal	$180	$180	$0
Student	$0	$0	$0
Credit card	$35	$35	$0
Credit card	$90	$90	$0
Credit card	$25	$0	+$25
Other	$0	$0	$0
	$330	**$305**	**+$25**

Taxes

Expense	Projected Cost	Actual Cost	Difference
Federal	$0	$0	$0
State	$0	$0	$0
Local	$0	$0	$0
Other	$0	$0	$0
	$0	**$0**	**$0**

Savings & Investments

Expense	Projected Cost	Actual Cost	Difference
Retirement account	$100	$100	$0
Investment account	$0	$0	$0
Other	$0	$0	$0
	$100	**$100**	**$0**

Gifts & Donations

Expense	Projected Cost	Actual Cost	Difference
Charity 1	$0	$0	$0
Charity 2	$0	$0	$0
Charity 3	$0	$0	$0
	$0	**$0**	**$0**

Legal

Expense	Projected Cost	Actual Cost	Difference
Attorney	$0	$0	$0
Alimony	$0	$0	$0
Payments on lien or judgement	$0	$0	$0
Other	$0	$0	$0
	$0	**$0**	**$0**

Budget Summary

EXPENSES

Projected expenses	$3,875
Actual expenses	$3,993
Difference	-$118

BALANCE

Projected balance	$325
Actual balance	$257
Difference	$68

Part Three:
Credit

CHAPTER *9*

Why Credit Is Important and When You Will Need It

Credit is the single most influential factor in determining how we live today. On a personal level, your credit tells a story about you to potential employers, insurance companies, banks, and schools. Your credit also impacts the ability to obtain necessities like a home, a car and make personal lifestyle choices.

Though credit is fully entrenched in our society most people know very little about it. After you read this section of *Life & Debt*, you will understand fully how and why credit works the way it does. You will know what your credit score is, what it means, how to manage it, how to get a copy of your credit report, and use it to successfully control your financial life. With these tools you will become your own personal credit expert.

BASIC CREDIT TERMS

Let's begin with explaining some terms:

1. Credit Report. A credit report is a detailed history of your credit information. It begins the first day you open a financial account in your name such as a bank account, student loan, or credit card. At that point you have created a credit history which will now become part of your ongoing credit report. It generally includes current information on balances and payment history of your various debts. There is information on mortgages, car loans, home equity loans, student loans, and credit cards, plus any negative credit reporting such as delinquent payments and bankruptcies. We will discuss these in more detail in the next chapter.

> **NOTE:** The history of any credit card you close will remain on your credit report for seven years.

Also — and this may surprise you — essential personal data such as your social security number, date of birth, employment history, and alias *(pg. 71)* are listed as well. So you can now see how important this report is, and how essential it is to keep an eye on it.

2. Credit Score. Anyone who has ever applied for a loan has heard about "checking their credit score" for eligibility. Generally it is a number based on everything in your credit report which instantly tells a potential creditor about you financially. One of the most popular scoring models used to calculate credit scores is called Fair Isaacs Corporation (FICO). Scores range from 300 to 850, and your score determines whether or not you will be considered for a car loan, a credit card, a mortgage, or any application you make for credit, and how much interest you will be charged. Like many things in life, the higher your score the better because it tells the lender the likelihood of being paid back for their loan. A score of 750 and above is generally considered top tier.

> **NOTE:** Please remember scores go up and down. If your score is low (600 and below) that does not mean you are a bad person — it just means you need help managing your debt and credit. Fortunately the *Life & Debt* system will do that for you.

3. Credit Bureaus. There are three major credit bureaus in the United States — Equifax, TransUnion, and Experian. Each keeps its own credit report for you based on information provided to them by your credit card and loan companies. This includes payment history, how much and how often you make payments and your balance on each. You are entitled to a free copy of your report every year from all three credit bureaus and I recommend you get each one. Your credit score can vary from bureau to bureau due to the fact that not all of your financial information, which is *supplied by creditors*, is reported to each one.

HOW CAN I CONTROL MY CREDIT SCORE?

I could write an entire book on that crucial question alone, and will explore this in depth throughout this section. Some of my clients tell me they don't care about their credit. I advise them they must if they want the things a good credit score can give them, which includes paying less for items that require a loan. Why? Lower interest rates come with a good credit score. The best way to control your credit score is to understand how it works, from getting copies of your credit report to checking your credit score on a regular basis.

Life & Debt teaches people how to be smart about their money and that means being *proactive* about their credit report and achieving a good credit score. My system gives you the tools to manage your debt, control your credit and lead a better life.

Life & Debt Tip

Get a copy of your credit report annually. To make it fun I suggest you choose October 31 — Halloween. You will not be scared because you will be in the know.

Alias and Your Credit

An alias may appear on your credit report as another version of your name which was used for credit received in the past. Examples include your maiden name, your name with a middle name or middle initial, or a prefix or suffix, like Dr. or Jr. It might be a nickname or a variation of your name. What you want to be very careful of is a credit report with the name of someone else listed. If an unknown name is listed as an alias on your report, that person may have applied for credit using your qualifications. You may also spot a version of your name that you have never used, such as one with your middle name or initial. If this occurs report the discrepancy — or any discrepancy — to the credit bureau where the alias appears. This is particularly important when you have a very common name, or you have the same name as other family members.

CHAPTER *10*

What Affects Your Credit?

Having good credit is essential to achieving financial and personal goals. There is nothing you can do, from applying for a new credit card or car loan, to making a late payment or filing for bankruptcy, that will not affect your credit score — and many things might surprise you.

Example: If you are shopping for a home loan, potential lenders could check your credit during this time period which could lower your score. Why? Because someone is looking at your credit history — past and present.

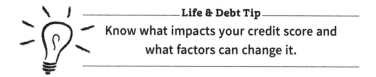

————Life & Debt Tip————
Know what impacts your credit score and
what factors can change it.

Harry's Story

One client, Harry G., came to me dumbfounded because he ended up with a delinquency on his credit report for a credit card he wasn't even using. A delinquency (explained later in this chapter) is serious and can cause a credit score to drop. It seems Harry applied for and activated a new credit card and then forgot about it because he never received his statements. A computer error sent them to the wrong address. You might assume that since he wasn't using the card a problem should not have occurred. Unfortunately his card had an annual fee, which began once the card was activated. However, since Harry wasn't receiving statements he could not pay the mounting fees. Had he been monitoring his credit report, he would have seen the delinquency and avoided the negative impact on his credit.

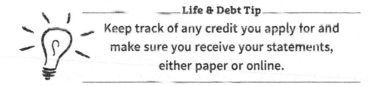

_____Life & Debt Tip_____
Keep track of any credit you apply for and make sure you receive your statements, either paper or online.

Credit Activity

Let's take a look at how your financial activities affect your credit score — positively and negatively. But first, it's important to keep in mind that determining credit scores is not an exact science. Many factors can impact your credit and some have nothing to do with your activity. Credit bureaus have their own criteria for evaluating you even though they are all using the same credit information. In general, each will determine your credit score based on five factors:

1. Previous credit performances
2. Current level of debt
3. Your credit history
4. Types of credit available
5. Requests for new credit

These factors will be explained in more detail in the next chapter.

HERE ARE SOME EXAMPLES OF ACTIONS THAT MAY IMPACT YOUR CREDIT

1. Opening a New Credit Card. Credit cards are part of our lives. When you apply for a new card, there is an inquiry on your credit report, causing your score to drop slightly. However, since scores continually fluctuate, that drop will not be permanent or affect your score severely.

> **NOTE:** Many people use credit cards to establish a credit history. However, this should be done in moderation. Do not succumb to the endless credit card offers that pack your mailbox. They create the potential for taking on more debt than you can manage.

2. Applying for a New Loan. Applying for a new loan will result in an inquiry on your credit report, which will lower your score. The impact could vary — from small to large — depending on the type of loan and how many inquiries were made during the loan application time frame. In the long run, the impact of a loan could be positive, especially if you pay on time.

3. Missing a Payment. A negative impact to your score will depend on which type of bill you missed a payment on and how long it was before you paid it. If it is a medical or utility bill, it may not impact your credit score unless you let it escalate and it goes to a collection agency. Once that happens it is reported to the credit bureaus. Do not let that happen. If you miss a payment on your credit card or a loan, you have until it is 30 days past due for the credit card company to report it.

4. Making a Late Payment. If you have gone beyond the 30-day grace period, even if you have paid the bill, it will be reported as a late payment, which will lower your score.

> **NOTE:** The later you pay, *(or don't pay at all),* the more it will negatively impact your score.

5. Closing a Credit Card. If you have 18 credit cards and want to get your get your credit in a different position by scaling down the number of cards, and your credit score is 620, then closing cards may not impact your credit. If you have three cards that are paid up, and a score of 720, you might see a small drop.

> **NOTE:** A small impact should never affect your decision to close cards. Scores go up and down all the time. Having 18 open cards creates its own negative impact on your finances and credit. It depends on your goal. If your goal is to take control of your credit and reduce the number of cards (no one needs 18 cards) then you take a small hit. You sometimes have to take a slight step back to step forward.

6. Credit History. Each line of credit you acquire, whether it's a credit card or mortgage, has a history of payments and balances. Potential lenders take a look at that history, accumulated during the time period of that particular credit. If you pay off a loan, or close a credit card, you do not immediately erase that history. Closed credit cards remain part of your history for seven years while a bankruptcy remains for 10 years. If you have an open credit card with a positive history of payments made on time, and a low balance, you might want to keep it open to show a potential lender you can manage a loan properly.

 7. High Credit Card Balances. The higher the balance on a credit card the more it will negatively impact your credit in comparison to the available credit line on that card. I suggest to my clients they try to use only 30% of the available credit, and *never* max-out a card, meaning do not use every dollar. Example if you have a credit line of $10,000, your balance should be $3,000, not $10,000. That is very negative. However, paying off the balance by using the card in moderation is always ideal.

8. A Variety of Loans. Having different types of loans on your report — credit card, mortgage, etc., is positive as long as you pay on time. That shows a lender you can handle various credit obligations.

9. Delinquency. Being delinquent with a payment, meaning you have gone past the grace period without paying, is very negative. It will be part of your credit history for seven years and the longer you are delinquent the greater the likelihood your debt will be sent to a collections agency, which will have an even greater negative impact.

10. Collection Agency. After being delinquent for a period of time your bill could be sent to a collection agency, which is organization that collects on delinquent debts. This will be reported and have a very negative impact. Never let things escalate to this stage. Legal action could follow collections, which will be reported, and further damage your credit and score.

11. Judgments. This means you have been sued for the money owed on a delinquent account and you lost. If you don't monitor your credit regularly you may not even know there is a judgment against you, especially if you have moved and never received lawsuit papers.

> **NOTE:** You are supposed to be notified when being sued but that doesn't always happen. The only way to be sure is to check your credit report and always know to whom you owe money.

12. Charge Off. This is an accounting term. It means the company you owe money to has moved your debt from column one marked "receivable" to column two marked "bad debt" in their books. They may decide you may never pay them and write it off, or sell it, or send it to a collection agency, or consider legal action. Because your debt is still on the books and being reported as a charge off, it will have a negative impact on your credit.

> **NOTE:** It is a common misconception that a charge off means you no longer owe the money.

13. Bankruptcy. Years ago if you filed for bankruptcy creditors loved you. You had no debt and a chance to borrow again — with them! Not today. It is one of the worst things you can do to your credit long term, and it could take 10 years to be removed from your credit report. However, people sometimes get in way over their heads, which I understand. Bankruptcy is an effective tool to relieve you of financial obligations, or help repay debts at a comfortable pace. That said, I caution the use of bankruptcy — and it's only to be considered as a last resort — as it will have a huge impact on your credit for years. It can affect future employment, licensing, insurance and if you are a business person, especially in banking or finance, you will be much less likely to be hired. It will be very, very difficult to get any kind of credit.

Diane's Story

Be very careful about asking someone to co-sign a loan. Diane G. did not have good enough credit to get a car loan so she asked a friend to co-sign it for her. Diane made regular payments but her friend then filed for bankruptcy. The car was listed as her friend's asset because she co-signed the loan. The result: despite making the payments, Diane lost the car and would never be repaid for the payments made. If Diane had monitored her credit score, and taken steps to establish a better credit history, she would never have been in a position to ask someone to co-sign a loan for her.

_____ Life & Debt Tip _____

Create a good credit history and monitor your credit regularly because there are too many variables which can impact your credit and score. Regular monitoring ensures you can maintain a good score by keeping an eye on accuracy.

CHAPTER *11*

The Next Level of Debt Collection

There are times when life can bring real hardships, such as a sudden job loss or serious illness, and these hardships can make paying bills very difficult. However, few people want to face the unpleasant consequences that come with chronic unpaid debt. Creditors have rights and I can assure you they will use those rights to collect any money you borrowed, plus the interest.

Laws vary from state to state but there are many ways creditors can seek repayment from you. They could start with phone calls and letters and, if unsuccessful in getting payment, send unpaid accounts to a collection agency. If your debts remain unpaid a downward spiral of further debt collection could begin. Trust me when I say that after more than 15 years of dealing with these serious issues, you do not want this to happen.

COLLECTIONS AND JUDGMENTS

We discussed collection agencies in Chapter 10, but basically if you do not meet your financial obligations, most creditors will eventually send your accounts to a collection agency. That agency's one goal is to get you to pay the debt you owe and will work hard to make it happen. Though tactics like harassing phone calls and inappropriate intimidation have lessened due to increased legal protection for consumers, the agency will pressure you for payment and could threaten to sue you and take you to court.

Being sued means your creditor has filed paperwork requesting a judge to order you to repay your debt. This places you far into the debt collection process. It is likely your credit has been negatively impacted and your creditor is getting closer to collecting what is owed by you along with interest and extra expenses such as court fees.

If after reviewing all the paperwork, the judge agrees with the creditor your debt becomes part of the public record and your creditor has a legal claim against you called a judgment. This is a legal determination by the judge that you are now a "judgment debtor" and owe your creditor (now a "judgment creditor") a certain amount of money. If you do not show up in court, which I do not recommend — you have a much better chance of pleading your case in person — the judge could order a default judgment against you.

A judgment is serious because it takes your case to the next level of debt collection and the unpleasant measures that come with it. These could include wage garnishment, freezing your bank accounts or seizing your property and you may not receive any prior notice.

> **NOTE:** Always consult with a lawyer or debt resolution expert before responding to any of these measures.

WAGE GARNISHMENT

If you are employed, wage garnishment is one of the first methods collectors will use to repay your debt after a judgment. If legal in your state, garnishment means a percentage of your wages will be deducted from your paycheck and sent to a sheriff or marshal acting as the collector for the collection agency. This will continue until the debt is repaid. Your employer will be notified but you cannot be fired due to wage garnishment.

You can object to wage garnishment by requesting a court hearing. A judge will then have to rule before your paycheck is garnished. You can also contact the creditor directly to try to work out a payment plan that does not involve garnishment. In my experience creditors who receive a wage garnishment are unlikely to work out a separate deal with you, however, it does not hurt to try.

During a wage garnishment, interest is still accruing on the debt and you could end up paying nearly double the original amount by the time you are finished.

The following is a list of income exempt from wage garnishment. If any of these are being garnished by your employer, ask a debt resolution expert for help:

- Public assistance
- Social Security
- Supplemental Security Income (SSI)
- Veterans benefits (VA)
- Child support

- Spousal maintenance
- Workers compensation
- Unemployment insurance

FREEZING BANK ACCOUNTS

If you have a checking or savings account, a creditor can serve your bank with a bank levy which is a notice ordering the bank to freeze the money in your accounts. The creditor will receive the funds levied from the bank and apply them toward repayment of your debt.

> **NOTE:** In some cases they will freeze double the judgment amount in the account. Some states have a minimum amount required to be left unfrozen, but the rest can be taken. Any outstanding checks will not clear, and any joint accounts with your social security number can also be accessed. This is a very scary scenario because it can happen without warning, and you can lose access to your money until the matter is resolved. There will also be a bank fee.

We generally advise you stay on top of delinquent debts and if you are sued seek professional help from an experienced debt resolution lawyer. It is in everyone's best interest — yours and your creditor's — to get these matters resolved. Even better, stop them before they start by following the *Life & Debt* rules of smart money management.

PROPERTY LIENS

Liens against your property are called judgment liens. To obtain one a judgment creditor files a lien against the property with the local records office. That means real property with your name on the deed has a lien against it and you cannot do anything with that property — refinance, transfer, or sell — until the lien on it has been satisfied or paid.

PROPERTY SEIZURE

A judgment creditor can obtain a "writ of execution" from the court to go after your personal property by instructing the sheriff or marshal to put a "levy" on it. A levy means your property — anything from a stamp collection to real estate or personal property in the home — can be confiscated by the officer and sold to pay the debt. Generally you will receive notice prior to this action and might be responsible for fees charged by the officer to perform it. Alternatively the officer instructs the holder of the property (in the case of real estate, or a car, that would be your bank) to turn it over to him. Your property is then sold at auction and applied to your debt.

Property that can be taken to satisfy a debt in certain circumstance:

- Home (when this happens it is a foreclosure. *See Homestead Exemptions, below.*)
- Car
- Household appliances (and large value items)
- Large-screen TV
- Or any other item of property that serves as security for a loan such as a diamond ring

Homestead Exemptions: Most states, but not all, have homestead exemptions, which are protections for debtors that prevent their home from being sold to satisfy debts held by judgment creditors. Homestead exemptions do not protect the family from foreclosure by the mortgage holder or another situation where the home serves as security for a loan.

CONSUMER RIGHTS IN CASES OF EXTREME DEBT COLLECTION

Fortunately you do have some rights when it comes to the extreme debt collection. The Fair Debt Collection Practices Act (FDCPA) is a federal consumer protection law that regulates what creditors can and cannot do. It also protects you from undue harassment by creditors. You can also contact the Federal Trade Commission or the Consumer Financial Protection Bureau. For more information, visit **www.ftc.gov.**

Many states have their own laws regarding creditor harassment that may vary from the FDCPA. To be sure of your legal rights contact your state Attorney General's office or Office of Financial Affairs.

It is important to remember that facing hard realities now, and not continuing to ignore delinquent debts as they get worse, — and they will only get worse — is your best course of action. You want options when resolving debts, and the longer you wait, and the deeper you get into any legal proceeding, the more limited your options will become. Nothing is insurmountable when it comes to debt resolution, and there is light at the end of the tunnel no matter how difficult situations become. Managing your finances and digging out of any deep hole is possible if you stay focused. Yes, your best defense is to try to make sure your financial troubles do not lead you into extreme debt collection. Following the *Life & Debt* system is a good way to ensure that does not happen.

CHAPTER *12*

What Is Your Credit Report, Your Credit Score and How to Get Copies of Each

In addition to budgeting, monitoring your credit report is an essential part of keeping your finances on track. A credit report is a detailed credit history compiled by private institutions called credit bureaus. Information on your credit history is given to businesses or creditors considering lending you money or credit, so they can evaluate your status as a potential borrower and determine any potential risks of doing business with you.

For these businesses and creditors to request information about you from a credit bureau, they must subscribe to that bureau. That said, individuals do not have access to your credit history without your permission, though employers and insurance companies do under certain circumstances.

In this chapter we will discuss your credit report, your credit score, and how to monitor both.

Your Credit Report

A credit report includes basic information such as your name, any aliases (also known as) used when applying for previous credit, current and former addresses, current and former employment, plus your credit history. A credit history lists all open credit accounts and their payment history, plus any reporting from collections agencies and public records such as bankruptcies, judgments, and tax liens.

> **NOTE:** Your payment history on any credit cards you have closed will remain on your report for seven years. This is also true of any loans. Bankruptcies remain on your report for 10 years.

The names, addresses, and the types of businesses for each of your creditors are listed along with account status — payment amounts, balance owed, and the terms of the credit. This is true whether the accounts are open or closed, current, or in default.

————————**Life & Debt Tip**————————
Understanding your credit report is an essential tool to maintaining good credit. I suggest you make friends with your credit reports and foster the relationship by checking them regularly for any inaccuracies.

Your credit report will not include information about your savings or checking accounts unless there is an overdraft — which is a line of credit from your bank. It will also not include information about gender, religion, ethnicity, medical history, political affiliation, or any criminal records.

> **NOTE:** Credit reports do not include your credit score but there are a number of ways to obtain them which I will discuss later in the chapter.

WHERE TO GET A COPY OF YOUR CREDIT REPORTS

There are three major credit reporting bureaus in the United States — Experian, TransUnion, and Equifax. I always recommend you get all three. Only by reviewing all three reports will you be able to have an accurate picture of your credit. Not all creditors subscribe to all three bureaus and report information to them, and your score can vary from bureau to bureau.

The result is that each credit report could contain different information about you and your financial history. Because reporting credit and loan history to any of the three bureaus is voluntary, not government mandated, there is no way to be sure of your complete credit standing, or correct any discrepancies, unless you have a copy of each.

CONTACT INFORMATION FOR EACH CREDIT BUREAU

According to the Fair and Accurate Credit Transactions Act of 2003, you are entitled to receive one free credit report annually from each of these bureaus. One reason for this was to address growing concerns about identity theft, which, in recent years, has become an increased threat.

Equifax
P.O. Box 740241, Atlanta GA 30374
800-685-1111
www.equifax.com

TransUnion

P.O. Box 2000, Chester PA 19022

800-680-7289

www.transunion.com

Experian

P.O. Box 2002, Allen TX 75013

888-397-3742

www.experian.com

THE FAIR CREDIT REPORTING ACT (FCRA)

The FCRA specifies who can access your report and why. You can obtain a free copy of your credit reports by contacting any of three credit bureaus, or by doing the following:

- Visit online **www.AnnualCreditReport.com**
- Or contact by mail at:
  Annual Credit Report Request Service
  P.O. Box 105281, Atlanta GA 30348-5281
- You can also call 877-FACTACT to reach the Annual Credit Report request line.

You will be asked to provide personal information to verify your identity. This will include your name, address, Social Security number, date of birth, and possibly a current or past credit payment such as your monthly mortgage amount, or the name of a creditor.

WHO CAN REQUEST A COPY OF YOUR CREDIT REPORT?

Legitimate lenders and merchants can purchase memberships with the three major credit bureaus to have quick access to your credit history when you apply for credit with them. For example, this is why you can be approved for a new retail store credit card in minutes.

Members are required to sign a contract with the credit bureau stating they will only review your credit report when they are considering you for new credit or loans, employment, or other legitimate business purposes. According to the FCRA any organization or person obtaining a copy of your credit report under false pretenses could be liable for a fine and up to one year in jail.

Organizations that can access your credit report include:

- Potential lenders and current lenders (credit cards, mortgage lenders, car loan companies, etc.)
- Landlords
- Insurance companies
- Government agencies and affiliates that provide government licenses or benefits
- State or local child support enforcement agencies

Organizations that (generally) need written permission to obtain your credit report include:

- Potential employers
- A person(s) authorized by you
- A person using your report to provide a service or product requested by you
- Companies you hire to monitor your credit reports

> **NOTE:** Once permission is given, that creditor retains the right to check your credit on a regular basis as a requirement for credit, providing this was stated in the initial agreement you signed with the institution.

Your Credit Score

Your credit score is a three-digit number based on information in your credit report. The most popular scoring model is called FICO and ranges from a low score of 300 to a high score of 850.

When you get your reports and subsequent scores I suggest you compare all very carefully. It is not uncommon for scores to vary between reports and by studying them over time you can begin to understand how scores are calculated.

HOW TO GET YOUR CREDIT SCORE

Unlike your credit reports you are not entitled to a free copy of your credit scores each year and if you want all three scores you will most likely have to purchase them.

The following are fee-based ways to obtain your credit scores:

1. Purchase them while ordering your credit report. Fees run from $10-$15 per score.

2. Subscribe to a credit monitoring service. I believe it is a good idea to use a credit monitoring service which will keep a close eye on your credit activity and provide reports and scores from all three bureaus on a regular basis. These services are subscription based and require a monthly fee which could run from $12-$20 per month. In addition to monitoring your credit, they will contact you any time anyone looks at your credit report.

The following are ways to obtain some of your credit scores for free:

1. Visit CreditKarma.com. They list one score: TransUnion.

2. Check your credit card statements. Some creditors are including a score on their statements.

3. If your application for a loan is denied you can request your score.

UNDERSTANDING HOW YOUR FICO SCORE IS CALCULATED

Since FICO is the most common scoring model, I will explain what criteria is used for determining your score. There are five factors which will have the biggest impact on your score. Become familiar with all five since you do have the ability to influence them

Key Scoring Factors

Payment History: 35%. Includes all payment history both positive and negative. Paying your bills on time is key to keeping your score high

Total Debt Owed: 30%. Using a high percentage of the various credit available to you can have a negative impact even if you are paying your bills on time. Example: If you have $10,000 in available credit and have used $8,000 it tells a potential creditor you are overextended and might have trouble paying your bills if they also extend you credit. This applies to all your available credit and creditors. If you have 20 credit cards all with balances close to your credit limit, you are overextended, which has a negative impact on your score.

Credit History Timeframe: 15%. Generally, a longer positive credit history will increase your credit score. Closing old credit cards and opening new ones will impact your credit history timeframe. If you have had a card for 20 years and then close it to open a new one that credit history is now closed.

Applying for New Credit: 10%. Applying for a variety of new credit in a short amount of time impacts your score, meaning every time you apply, an inquiry by the potential lender appears on your report. The more inquiries, the lower your score.

Types of Credit: 10%. This means the variety of credit you have such as credit cards, car loans, mortgages, store cards, student loans, etc. Certain types of credit make more of an impact than others. For example a credit card with a $500 limit will not have the same impact as a car loan which you have been paying for 18 months. This is because a car loan is secured (by the car) and a credit card is not.

WHY A CREDIT SCORE IS IMPORTANT

Credit scores can change in an instant. Your score today could be different tomorrow based on new reporting from creditors or potential creditors. So why is your score important and why all the hype? Unless you intend to pay cash for everything — and few people can do that — knowing your score, and keeping it as high as possible, puts you in the best possible position to be considered for a credit card, a loan, and the interest you will pay.

Also, your score is often weighed against other people, meaning you are placed in a credit tier (see following box). People with Tier 1 credit scores get the best rates for their loans and pay less for the things they need in life, and who doesn't want that?

If your credit score is not Tier 1, do not worry, that's why you are reading this book. There was a time when I had a mountain of student loans that I could not pay, and no credit history — that is not Tier 1 by any means. I turned that around by taking charge of my budgets and credit. With my *Life & Debt* system I now teach people how to achieve the same positive results — and that includes you.

The Next Steps

Embracing and understanding the information on your credit reports is all part of making the *Life & Debt* system work for you. The details in these reports will affect your daily financial life and you will be surprised how easy it is to learn how to check them for errors and discrepancies. In the next chapter I will show you what is in your reports, what's important, and what isn't, and how to correct any errors.

CHAPTER *13*

How to Read Your Credit Report

Managing your debt begins with creating and maintaining a budget and continues with regular monitoring of your credit report. Because a credit report keeps you up-to-date on your debt, you can more easily devise a budget for paying it off *and* resist the temptation to take on more.

Order copies of your credit reports *at least* once a year. This allows you to take control of your credit, and credit score, by checking for inaccuracies, potential fraud and to see what impacts your credit both favorably and unfavorably. In this chapter I will describe the various sections of a standard credit report and show you how to read them.

See *Appendix II* for a sample credit report.

Credit Report Sections

Credit reports will vary depending on which of the three major credit reporting bureaus — Experian, TransUnion, or Equifax — is compiling them.

However, in general, they are organized in four separate sections:

1. Personal or Identifying Information
2. Credit History
3. Public Records
4. Inquiries

PERSONAL INFORMATION

As stated earlier, personal information will include your name, any aliases (also known as), social security number, date of birth, current and former addresses, current and former employers, and other data depending on circumstances.

CREDIT HISTORY

Your credit history will be a detailed listing of all your creditors, the type of credit you have with each creditor (you might have a mortgage and a credit card with one bank) and the account number of each. For security purposes, the full account number may not be listed, but it will clarify what type of credit the account is. For example, a mortgage may be listed as a home, an installment credit, or revolving credit.

> **NOTE:** Installments mean fixed payments where revolving credit payments can vary.

It can include whether the account is under your name only or joint names, the credit limit on the account, your current balance, whether you pay a fixed amount each month, if it has a minimum monthly balance, the payment history and whether the account is active, closed, or paid off. A comments portion might state the status of the account meaning whether it was closed by you, sent to a collections agency, charged off, in default, or current.

PUBLIC RECORDS

This section lists any bankruptcies you have filed, judgments from the court, or tax liens. Criminal activities, arrests, or lawsuits are not included.

INQUIRIES

An inquiry is the term used for any request to check your credit report. There are two kinds, hard and soft inquiries. A hard inquiry occurs when you make a request for a new line of credit such as applying for a new credit card. As previously explained *(pg. 74)*, this will impact your credit score to a degree. A soft inquiry does not impact you credit. Examples of a soft inquiry include requesting a copy of your credit report, companies that want to prescreen you for credit offers, potential employers, or current creditors monitoring your account.

CREDIT REPORT SUMMATION

Credit reports usually have a summary section of all the above information. Credit bureaus use proprietary codes for their summations so make sure you review the coding guidelines which are included with your report.

What to Do If You Find a Mistake

Reporting mistakes or inconsistencies is one of the main reasons for carefully checking your credit reports. If you see something, like a credit account that is not yours, or an account with the wrong financial information, immediately contact the credit bureau to file a dispute. Your report will list contact information which includes a phone number to reach a credit bureau representative. You will also be able to download a dispute application form online and send to the bureau via certified mail. Make sure you make copies of everything before you go to the post office. I also suggest you obtain copies of all your reports to see if the error exists on one or all three.

If you have not received a reply to your dispute within 30 days, call to follow-up and make sure they are investigating. The credit bureau should contact the creditor you listed as being in error. Your dispute will be listed on your credit report until it is resolved.

Credit Monitoring Services

Signing up for a credit monitoring service, which can keep tabs on your credit for you, is a good option for people who may be too busy to remember to check their credit reports and credit scores regularly. In addition to various independent businesses offering this service, many credit card companies do as well. You still have to review everything very carefully, but they provide regular reports and scores from all three bureaus and will contact you anytime anyone looks at your credit. They are generally subscription based with fees ranging from $12 to $20 per month.

Fraud Alerts and Security Freezes

You are entitled to place a free fraud alert on your credit reports for 90 days. This is advisable in the age of identity theft, and a useful tool. Let's say you receive a notice from a company of a data breach where your personal information was stolen and now might be used to open credit accounts in your name. A fraud alert to the credit bureaus will flag your report if a new application for credit is submitted and make it harder to be a victim of identity theft. A business must verify your identity before it issues credit. A fraud alert to one of the three bureaus will be shared with the other two and allows you to order a free copy of your credit report from each.

A security freeze can also be placed on your account. Unlike a fraud alert you will need to contact each of the three credit bureaus separately to place a freeze on your credit. Fees vary but expect to pay about $10 for a 90-day freeze. Your credit report will not be shared with anyone including potential creditors, employers, and insurance companies without your permission first. However, your current creditors will still have access to your report, and you can still check it. It will prevent new credit accounts from being opened in your name.

> **NOTE:** A security freeze can be temporarily lifted by you, or removed by you, at any time.

To place a security freeze on your credit complete the following steps:

1. Contact your state attorney general's office to inquire about placing a freeze on your credit. Be sure to ask them how much it costs and how long it will last.

2. Contact the three major credit bureaus: Experian, TransUnion and Equifax.

Military Members and Active Duty Alerts

If you are a member of the military deployed away from home, one way to not worry about identity theft and credit fraud is to put an "Active Duty Alert," or a security freeze on all three credit bureaus prior to leaving. Any businesses or potential creditors will then have to verify your identity before any new credit can be issued in your name. You can designate a personal representative to act on your behalf. An active duty alert will be in effect for one year and will reduce the number of pre-approved credit solicitations for two years.

To place a security freeze on your credit complete the following steps:

1. Contact your state attorney general's office to inquire about placing a freeze on your credit. Be sure to ask them how much it costs and how long it will last.

2. Contact the three major credit bureaus: Experian, TransUnion, and Equifax.

If You Suspect Identity Theft

If, after carefully reviewing your credit report, you find credit card charges you do not recognize, or have a higher debt balance then your records show, you may be a victim of identity theft. If so, the first step is to contact your creditors and request information about your account including a statement. Review your statements and any documentation with the company and dispute any inaccurate charges. Place a *fraud alert* or a *security freeze* on your credit report *(see details, pg. 98)* which will help protect your credit from further fraudulent activity. Remember to review reports from all three credit bureaus and file any disputes you find with each bureau.

The next step is to officially report any fraudulent activity by filing a complaint with the Federal Trade Commission (FTC) at **www.ftc.gov/complaint**, or by calling 877-438-4338. You should then file a police report as a victim of identity theft. Keep a copy of the report with the report number for your records. Identity theft is serious.

TIPS FOR PREVENTING IDENTITY THEFT

As more people share personal date online, identity theft is an ever-growing threat. Placing a fraud alert or a security freeze on your credit after you are alerted to a security breach is correct, but the following could minimize your risk before the fact.

1. Shred all documents with personal information before putting them in the garbage.

2. Be wary of unfamiliar online sites that require sensitive and personal data such as social security numbers and

credit card numbers upon registration. With e-commerce sites that require payment information check to see if their URL — that begins in http — has a picture of a lock.

3. Check your credit reports to make sure the account numbers match on your credit cards.

4. Carefully review all credit card statements — paper or online — to check for fraudulent charges.

5. Use complex passwords with a combination of upper and lower case letters, plus numbers.

Mario's Story

Mario B. came to see me because his overall financial situation was becoming bleak and he was struggling to pay his bills. Even though he thought he was aware of his debts and the accounts to which he owed money, his hours at work had been cut and he was taking home less money while his expenses were increasing. Since he had not checked his credit report recently I suggested we "pull" a free copy from each of the three credit bureaus to confirm his account balances.

He was surprised at how easy it was to obtain the reports, and very glad we did because we found two inconsistencies. One was an account he had forgotten about due to sloppy paperwork but the other was much more serious. Someone had opened a fraudulent account in his name and without his permission, meaning he was a victim of identity theft. I suggested he dispute the fraudulent account with the credit bureau, file a police report and put a credit freeze on his credit reports until the matter was cleared up. Luckily the fraudulent account was removed before too much damage was done to his finances and his credit score. Mario learned that even though paying bills can become very stressful when money is tight, it is crucial to stay in control of your finances, and that means checking your credit reports.

Life & Debt Tip

The combination of budgeting and credit monitoring is the best way to manage your debt and keep your finances on track.

CHAPTER *14*

Myths and Facts About Credit

The following are some of the most common myths surrounding credit and credit scores. Credit is easily misunderstood by many people but after reading *Life & Debt* you will not be one of them. Now that you have read through the detailed chapters on credit, I have compiled these as a quick and easy resource.

MYTH: Closing a lot of credit cards will improve my credit score.
FACT: Closing many cards at once can have a negative impact on your score because the ratio of your debt to your available credit will be smaller by removing cards with credit. For example if you have $10,000 in debt and $20,000 in available credit, closing a few cards drops your available credit to $5,000, which changes your debt to credit ratio. You can definitely close a credit card, but it is a bad idea to close to many in a short period of time. It

is better to pay off the balances on your cards and put them in a drawer and not use them, instead of closing them. This way you preserve a positive credit history on your credit report. However, make sure you request the statements anyway to check for fraudulent activity.

> **NOTE:** If closing credit cards is part of your overall plan to take charge of your credit, then the small impact on your score may be worthwhile to reach your goals.

MYTH: Opening new credit will hurt my score.
FACT: Applying for new credit may lower your score by a few points temporarily, but in most cases if your new credit is used responsibly it can have a positive impact on your score in the long run.

MYTH: Checking my credit report or credit score will reduce my score.
FACT: No! Checking your credit report is considered a soft inquiry meaning it has no impact on your credit. You can check your credit reports as often as you'd like, although you can only get a free report once a year. When a potential lender, such as a credit card company or bank, is offering you a loan and looks at your credit report it is considered a hard inquiry that will generally cost you a few points off your score.

MYTH: My income affects my credit score.
FACT: No! Your income affects your ability to pay your bills but it has no effect on your credit score. Your employer may appear on your credit report, but your income will not. Your credit report also doesn't include information such as gender, ethnicity, religion, political affiliation, medical history, or criminal records.

MYTH: I don't have to worry about my credit score because my significant other has a good score.

FACT: This is a bad motto to live by. There are many loans, like mortgages, which may require checking the credit scores of both spouses. If one score is low it can have a negative impact on the interest rate and terms of the loan. Also, if your spouse runs into financial trouble it will be difficult to get credit if both of you have low scores. Lastly, if you divorce, end your relationship, or your spouse passes away, you will have to consider what your score is by yourself.

MYTH: With a bad credit score I can never get a loan.

FACT: This is not necessarily true. There are many companies willing to give loans to people with low scores. However, the interest rate will most likely be much higher than someone with good or excellent credit.

> **NOTE:** Be aware of "predatory lending" offers where loan amounts and repayment terms — like interest rates — are very high.

MYTH: Bad credit never goes away.

FACT: Not true! If you pay off delinquent accounts and use your accounts responsibly you will start to see your score improve. A credit score is just a snapshot of your current financial status and responsibilities and can always go up or down. Check your credit reports to see how long certain negative activity will stay listed on them. Generally, bankruptcies stay for 10 years while debts placed for collection stay for seven years.

> **NOTE:** You can improve bad credit. It may take some time but you can do it.

MYTH: How I manage my personal checking bank accounts, investments and other personal finances has an impact on my score.

FACT: Your bank account is not linked to your credit report unless you have an overdraft, neither are any investment accounts or anything paid in cash. However, make sure all accounts are closed properly and monthly fees do not remain charged to your account. Unpaid fees can end up at a collection agency and on your report.

MYTH: I pay my bills on time so I have good credit.

FACT: Paying bills on time is very important to having good credit but other factors come into play. For good credit, your payment history, the amount of your debt, the age of your credit history, any new credit inquiries, and the types of credit you have are all factors. Any can lower your credit score, even if you pay bills on time.

MYTH: I believe I have good credit.

FACT: Believing and knowing are not the same thing. The best way to know the status of your credit is to get regular copies of your credit reports. Also if you had good credit a year ago that does not mean you still do — all the more reason to stay on top of your reports.

MYTH: I have no credit accounts so I have good credit.

FACT: If you have no credit or credit history, potential creditors will not look favorably on you as a potential borrower because there is nothing to show them how you have handled debt. If you plan on taking out a loan anytime soon, it's best to open up a line of credit, like a credit card, be responsible with the payments, and build a favorable credit history.

MYTH: Disputing credit accounts will make it come off of my report.

FACT: This is not always true. If you dispute an account with the credit bureau they will investigate the claim. If they find the account or information is inaccurate, or the creditor does not respond to the inquiry, they will generally remove the error. However, if they find it is accurate and your responsibility, they will *not* remove the account from your report.

MYTH: I don't need to worry about my credit report because I will not be applying for any new credit.

FACT: This may be true during certain times of your life, but you do have to worry about your credit because both insurance companies and potential employers do check it. Therefore, if you have a great score it will help your chances of getting a job or a better insurance rate. If you have bad credit it will hurt both. Also, interest rates on current credit cards and insurance premiums will differ based on your score. You never know if you might need a loan for a new car or a home or a new line of credit so you should always monitor your credit and practice good financial habits to keep it a positive score.

MYTH: Scores are locked in for six months.

FACT: Your score changes as soon as data on your credit report changes. Scores are not locked — they are calculated on a day-to-day basis.

MYTH: I just got divorced and the agreement says my ex has to pay the debts, but they are in my name so I don't have to worry about my credit.

FACT: If the debt was incurred as a joint account, both spouses are responsible to pay it back. If one doesn't follow the agreement, the other will suffer the consequences of an unpaid debt. Creditors do not have to notify you if your ex is late on a payment or has defaulted on a debt. Do not leave your credit in someone else's hands. If the debt has your name on it, but your ex is responsible for the payments, I strongly suggest you arrange to have the money given to you first so you can pay the creditor.

MYTH: I can always go to a credit repair agency to fix my credit.
FACT: There are companies that claim they can fix bad credit, but they can only repair your credit if there are some discrepancies or errors with your accounts. If this doesn't apply to you, or you have only experienced some bad credit habits in the past, these services are probably a waste of time and money.

Part Four:

The Next Steps

CHAPTER *15*

The Many Benefits of *Life & Debt*

In this final section of *Life & Debt* it is now time to reap the rewards of your efforts and see how embracing your debt really pays off. Throughout the course of this book I have shown you how to rethink the word debt to make it work for you, plus taught you the value of budgeting and monitoring your credit. These are the essential tools in the *Life & Debt* system.

First let's do a quick review of what you have learned so far:

THE BASIC TOOLS OF *LIFE & DEBT*

Embrace Your Debt. In our society we all need debt so it is much better to understand it and embrace it then to be fearful of it. By knowing the difference between good debt and bad debt you can now better manage your finances and make informed decisions about income, expenses, and lifestyle choices.

The healthier your overall financial picture is, the happier you will be. You can now feel empowered by your debt, and enjoy the many benefits of "a beautiful friendship."

Learn to Budget. Learning how to budget is the primary tool in the *Life & Debt* system of debt management. Organizing your finances through budgeting will help you better understand your money and bills. With my standard monthly budget *(pg. 62)* you have learned how much money is coming in each month (income) and how much is coming out (expenses). You now can make better decisions about where and how that money is spent, saved, and invested. More detailed budgets give you the freedom to acquire specific lifestyle expenses.

You also have learned that sometimes "tough love" is the best approach to achieving financial security and cutting a few things out of your budget to reach your goals is really not as painful as imagined.

MONITOR YOUR CREDIT REPORT AND CREDIT SCORE

Credit Report. I have stressed that ordering and studying your credit report once a year is also essential to the *Life & Debt* system. It is the mirror image of your financial health and will quickly tell you if your budgeting has been successful. Study your report and target the areas that need work. Start relying less on credit cards and more on cash. Have an emergency fund ready. Pay down the balances of your highest interest rate cards and try to keep a few in your wallet. Your credit report is a guide to meeting these financial goals now and in the future.

> **NOTE:** This will be discussed in Chapter 17, "Breaking the Credit Card Addiction."

Credit Score. We discussed credit scores at length in Chapter 12. They are snapshots of your current credit status *(see Tier system on pg. 93)* and can change daily. Because they go hand-in-hand with managing your debt I also showed you several ways to obtain your credit scores. You may be saying 'I already have a good credit score.' Trust me when I say there are no assurances unless you check. It has been reported that one in three Americans have a collection matter reported on their credit report and do not even know about it.

Also, life happens. Unforeseen issues, or loss of income, are some of the many ways your credit score can be instantly impacted in a negative way. Because you now are fully informed about your score it will help you protect and nurture it so you can resolve problems before they happen.

THE ESSENTIAL BENEFITS OF *LIFE & DEBT*

Financial Freedom. Can you imagine what financial freedom really feels like? How about sleeping through the night, less arguing with your significant other about money, or less stress about earning money. All this can happen with *Life & Debt*. You can embrace your financial life, and even love it, with my tools and a good attitude. Life is simple when you don't have to worry about debt — so is managing your finances. Instead of worrying about money, you'll have extra funds to be able to save for your future. You will have that wonderful freedom that comes with financial security.

Less Stress. Stress and debt go hand in hand, which I have observed many times when clients first enter my office. Stress is often caused by "robbing Peter to pay Paul," which does not solve the actual problem — a continuous cycle of borrowing

— or resolve your difficulties with debt management. I assure you that if you follow my *Life & Debt* system you will lower your bills and learn to end the cycle of debt. Once both are done, this will go a long way to easing stress throughout your life.

Looking to the Future with Happiness, Not Fear. Once you remove the constant worry about money and debt, you can start thinking about what you want today, tomorrow, and in the next five years. You can plan for your family's needs now and then. *Life & Debt* allows you to make a working plan to reach financial goals and be happy while doing it. As said, eliminating debt also will help prepare for the unexpected. You can start funding a "what if" fund so next time you have a home repair, your car breaks down, or have a medical bill your insurance won't cover, you don't have to worry about.

In short, *Life & Debt* is a win-win for you, your family, and your future.

CHAPTER *16*

Debt Reduction

In our society, acquiring debt is relatively easy. However, when you get in too deep, resolving it is not. In this chapter I will discuss various types of debt resolution options and services — what they do, what you need to know before choosing one, and how it will impact your credit.

What to Do Prior to Debt Resolution

Do Your Homework. Though I have been helping clients successfully resolve their debt for more than 15 years, it still surprises me when I hear of people who sign up for debt resolution through a telemarketer or by clicking an online ad. Being deeply in debt is scary, but don't let your fear take you from the frying pan into the fire. Do your homework and research all companies before you give them your business. Here are some suggestions:

1. Contact the Better Business Bureau to see if any complaints have been filed against them, how many, and if they have been resolved. Complaints happen. The key is what the company did about it. You can also contact your state attorney general's office.

2. Check to see if they are licensed in your state to practice debt resolution, and for how long. You can do this online at your state department of finance or bankruptcy department.

3. You can research companies online as long as you are very thorough about it and go to as many credible sites as possible to make informed comparisons. Also make sure the company has a physical address, not just an online presence.

Frances' Story

When Frances M. came to see me, she had already spoken to another debt resolution professional, but was still on the verge of declaring bankruptcy. With $40,000 in debt, she said she had been given no viable alternatives except bankruptcy. Frances was feeling guilty about not being able to pay her monthly bills, and the thought of bankruptcy was making her guilt and shame much worse. First I explained to her there is no shame in considering bankruptcy. For some it is a viable option, but fortunately she would not have to use this option. Frances was greatly relieved when I was able to rework her existing budget to resolve her debt without bankruptcy.

Whether you are deeply in debt like Frances, or nervous about losing control of your finances, it helps to know there are many debt resolution options. Do not let fear stop you from doing your research and asking for professional advice. Take a step back and proceed with a clear head and know there are options and answers for your finances now and in the future.

Debt Resolution Services

1. Attorneys or Law Practices

If you decide to seek an attorney make sure their primary business is debt resolution. That is my practice exclusively, so when clients come to me they know they are hiring a proven expert. As said, make sure the attorney is licensed to work in the state where you reside, and only use a firm that will meet with you in person without a consultation fee. Ask them how long they have been in practice. Like many things in life, experience counts. Someone with a lengthy track record already has connections to your creditors and knows how to work with them.

2. Debt Counseling/Credit Card Counseling

These are non-profits organizations which can help you devise budgets and create a management plan to pay down your debt. Ask for suggestions from your local legal aid service or through local charities or religious affiliations. Confirm their exact services before you move forward.

3. Debt Settlement

This is a company or individual that will claim to be able to resolve your debt for less then what you owe. Be very careful because there are plenty of fraudulent companies looking to take your money and not do the job. Make sure they are properly licensed in your state (this varies from state to state, but try researching the state department of finances or banking department). Only hire a company that will meet with you personally first, does not charge fees upfront, and has a longstanding and positive reputation.

4. Debt Consolidation

This is when you take out one large loan to pay off your multiple debts. Generally it consolidates them all into one monthly payment and is perfect for those who find it easier to manage a one payment method. You may also get an added bonus — sometimes a large loan has lower interest rates. However, be careful not to rob Peter to pay Paul. Know if it's eliminating your debt, or simply changing form. Meaning, make certain the new consolidated debt is structured to help you pay down the debt.

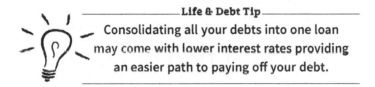

Life & Debt Tip

Consolidating all your debts into one loan may come with lower interest rates providing an easier path to paying off your debt.

5. Bankruptcy

I always advise bankruptcy as a last resort. The only time it is a good fit is when you have literally no assets or income to pay off your debt. Generally there are two types of bankruptcy for consumers: Chapter 7 and Chapter 13. I suggest you hire an attorney to facilitate this process and be aware there are numerous fees. Also beware that a bankruptcy will have a serious impact on your credit, and will stay on your credit reports for 10 years.

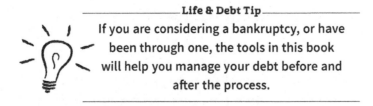

Life & Debt Tip

If you are considering a bankruptcy, or have been through one, the tools in this book will help you manage your debt before and after the process.

Most Common Types of Personal Bankruptcies

Chapter 7: This is a liquidation. In general, all your debts are in effect wiped out.

Chapter 13: Here you work with your creditors to restructure your debt balances and set up payment plans to pay them back. Some of your overall debt may be forgiven, but you could still end up paying back the full amount.

How Debt Resolution Impacts Your Credit and Credit Reports

Many of my clients are fearful of how debt resolution impacts their credit scores. Yes, eliminating debt will impact your credit and credit scores in the short term, but in the long term the impact is positive. It is helpful to keep the big picture in mind.

How debt resolution impacts your credit is based on a number of factors — some of which may seem surprising. If you have an excellent credit score (750+), and your accounts are in good standing, you may take a bigger hit to your credit if you stop paying your credit cards to resolve debt for less than what you owe, than someone who already has a low score due to delinquency.

Because debt settlement does attempt to pay off the entire balance it could impact your score negatively because your credit report will state the debt was not paid in its entirety.

However, paying less than the full amount owed is still a step forward in resolving your debt, and allows you to move toward a better place financially.

As discussed, a bankruptcy has serious consequences — your score will fall, it will stay on your credit reports for 10 years, and you may not be able to secure a loan for years afterwards. The bottom line is you really need an expert to carefully evaluate your entire financial situation and offer choices, benefits, and consequences before proceeding with a bankruptcy plan.

It is important to remember that negative reporting on your credit can be followed by positive reporting. Just because you found yourself in over your head does not mean it has to stay that way. The best way to bring your credit score back up after debt resolution is to use the tools in this book to understand and embrace your debt, setup and follow regular budgets, and monitor your credit.

CHAPTER *17*

Breaking the Credit Card Addiction

Addiction to credit cards is a very real problem. Often clients come into my office with wallets filled with 20 or more credit cards. Fortunately the *Life & Debt* system has a "Six-Step" program to help. Like many addictions, it is tough to beat. However, once you take that first step, you are on your way to relieving the burden of "bad" debt, and securing a better financial future.

Life & Debt's Six-Step Program to Break Credit Card Addiction

1. Recognize the Problem. When you are deeply in credit card debt and truly desperate due to your financial troubles, it is time to face hard realities — using too many credit cards are the problem and "withdrawal" is necessary. There are many reasons why people fall into debt — stress, fear, economic disaster — but you can break the credit card addiction and you *will* be happier for it.

The following are clear indicators you have a problem:

- You have no available credit on your credit cards so you cannot purchase anything with them.

- You are afraid to look at your bills.

- There is no money in your bank accounts at the end of the month.

2. Just Say No. The credit card companies want your business, and once you get on their lists you will be flooded with incentives for more cards offering short-term benefits like low interest rates on balance transfers. It's very enticing but for those with credit addiction it is dangerous. An easy way to "just say no" to more cards is to immediately place unsolicited mail from potential creditors right in the trash and accept no more "on the spot" offers of store credit cards, no matter how attractive the discounts are. This way you stop the vicious cycle of more debt.

3. Downsize Your Credit Cards. Many people are so attached to their credit cards (particularly retail store cards) they can't dream of parting with them. Trust me, you can, and life *will* go on. I had one client, Amanda, who was a tough case even for me. She had a card from a very expensive specialty store that she coveted — there is no other way to describe it. With that card she could binge on ridiculously pricy items that could be found for a fraction of the cost in other stores. There is nothing wrong with making choices, but her binging was seriously jeopardizing her family's finances. I had to "run the numbers" several times and place the before / after lists in front of her before she finally understood what she was doing.

> **NOTE:** Amanda survived this "tough love" approach, and though she still has issues, her need for this credit card has ended.

4. Put Your Credit Cards in a Drawer for One Week. That's right, put your credit cards in a drawer for one week and see how you do. Keep your debit card handy, but see how many times you would reach for a credit card in the course of a week. If you don't have it in your wallet, then you have the ability to determine if the purchase is an impulse buy, or something really necessary. After one week, sort through the cards you left in the drawer and choose one to keep in your wallet for emergencies for one month. If after a month those other cards do not leave the drawer, you have learned you do not need them either. Choose one or two to put in your wallet and get rid of the rest.

> **NOTE:** Prepaid cards are an alternative.

5. Start Relying on Cash or Debit Cards. In our society there are many myths about the necessity for credit cards — many of which are untrue. In general, whatever you can do with a credit card, like renting a car or booking a hotel room, can be done with a debit card. You may need a utility bill for proof of address but that is not difficult. Because you now know how to use the *Life & Debt* budget system in Chapter 5, you can rely more on using cash and debit cards to pay monthly expenses instead of charging yourself deeper into debt.

6. Maintain a Healthy Balance of Credit and Debt. Relying solely on credit is a thing of the past. Today, it is more important to have cash in the bank for emergencies, and the security that comes with knowing you have money to fall back on. The *Life & Debt* system has shown you how to budget and monitor your credit so you can break the credit addiction. Ideally your cash reserves in a bank account should cover at least six months' worth of regular expenses based on your budget, and you should maintain one or two credit cards with low balances, or no balances.

Jules' Story

My client Vivian C. came to me for help with her daughter Jules, a college student who got in way over her head with credit card debt. During her first semester at college Jules received an unsolicited credit card offer and promptly opened the account. Though the maximum credit limit was relatively low — $500 — it was enough to trigger a spending spree. More credit cards offers followed, all opened by Jules who maxed them out to the tune of $15,000 without understanding or considering the consequences. That is until she realized that making late payments or no payments (she had no income) did not pay down the balances, it just made them much bigger. She eventually got scared and rightly so.

When Vivian learned her daughter had a maxed out 13 credit cards with no means to pay the bills, she was furious. At that time Vivian was a single mom working three jobs to make ends meet and really needed my help. First I worked on a budget to allow Vivian to pay down her daughter's debt which took four years. Next I taught Jules the "just say no" response to any credit card offers, which means tossing them in the trash. I then taught her how to budget and use an ATM for purchases — no credit cards.

The moral here is you need to know your credit card limits. Credit card companies send offers to people hoping they will accept the cards, use them and accumulate debt. Also, banks make a lot of money when you only pay the minimum. Do not think you are getting something for free. Debt is a part of life, but it is never free, which Jules was too young to realize at the time but certainly understands now.

Conclusion

In general, you will probably always have some form of debt, and a credit card, but you are now able to manage both successfully. Breaking addictions is not easy, but you have taken control and that is a great feeling. Enjoy it.

Life & Debt Tip

If you believe you have an addiction to spending or acquiring too many credit cards, contact Debtors Anonymous. They are there to help.
www.debtorsanonymous.org

CHAPTER *18*

Planning for the Unexpected

If there is only enough money in your checking account to pay your bills at the end of the month and anything extra — or unexpected — is paid for with credit cards, you are skating on the edge of financial disaster. This means it is time to rethink your financial strategy. I can assure you there is a way off the edge of financial disaster and the bad debt that comes with it. One of the many benefits of the *Life & Debt* system is that it not only shows you how to break the cycle of debt, but how to rethink your money, manage your finances, and plan for the unexpected. Just like being your own creditor, planning means putting money away (as part of your budget) for your "what if" fund.

Why a "What if" Fund Is Essential

It's easy to get caught up in the credit card debt cycle encouraged by our consumer-driven society. However, getting out of debt also means planning for the unexpected. The two are linked. Your first financial obligation is to pay your monthly expenses, which are subjective, meaning we choose which bills are priorities. Yet, no matter how carefully we plan our lives and budgets, things happen. They can also occur when we are least prepared for them such as a major car repair, a flood in the basement, a job lay-off, or new medical considerations. Just like preparing for a big storm by stocking up on food, batteries and water, you need to have your "what if" fund ready and waiting.

Not to say all unexpected expenses are unhappy or negative. A client told me of a family whose set of triplets are all getting married at the same time at the same event. This is a wonderful occasion for the family and a celebration for their friends. However, wedding gifts can be pricy and guests at that wedding will need to buy three gifts at once. If there is no room in their budget, and they have to fall back on credit cards, it will be a very expensive occasion in more ways than one. In short they are not prepared for the "what if" scenario.

In each section of this book I have stressed the need for savings. I have shown you how to take control of your monthly income and expenses and set up a working budget in Chapter 6. Part of that budget includes savings. Without it you will be "caught short" every time an unexpected expense or emergency occurs and fall back on credit cards. I have discussed the necessity for monitoring your credit and how to break the credit card addiction *(pg. 120)*.

> **NOTE:** There are many people who believe they must have credit cards "just in case" for emergencies or a "what if" scenario. What they need is to work on their mind set. Many of my clients, who have successfully rethought their views on money and cash, have told me they cannot believe how much they *once* relied on credit cards.

You do not need a credit card for emergencies, I assure you, if you rethink the process of reaching for a card every time there is a "what if" situation. Reach for cash instead and your *Life & Debt* situation will be more manageable.

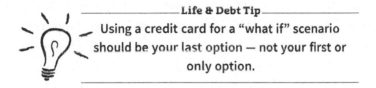

Life & Debt Tip

Using a credit card for a "what if" scenario should be your last option — not your first or only option.

HOW TO START A "WHAT IF" FUND

1. Set Reasonable Goals. As the saying goes, "From small things big things come," and this is true of savings. If you save $10 a week from your paycheck, (the cost of two lattes) in one year you will have $520. Double it and you will have $1,040 ready cash. Another tried and true starter system is to throw all your loose change at the end of the day into a classic "spare change jar". Trust me, you will never miss the change and it can really mount up. I was told of someone who ended up with $300 in one year. Also, turning coins into dollars is easy because there are coin redemption machines everywhere these days. Just think about how good it will feel to know you can now afford an expensive gift or a new appliance.

2. Open a Savings Account. At the end of your first month of saving take your cash directly to the bank and open a special savings account. This account will now be your "what if" fund which is cash on hand for emergencies, special gifts or purchases. No need to immediately fall back on credit cards which only accrue more bad debt. Keep your credit cards in a drawer and remember to pay yourself as a creditor, meaning make regular payments to your savings account.

3. Make Regular Contributions to Savings until You Reach 10% of Net Income. Once you get in the habit of putting money aside, increase the amounts you deposit in your savings each month. Ideally you can aim for 10% of your net income (take-home pay) to go into your new savings account. In time you can have six-months' worth of expenses ready if needed. Imagine how wonderful you will feel knowing you are finally covered if an emergency happens, or that dream vacation you always wanted can come true after all. The bottom line is this — you have cash on hand if you need it without accruing more bad debt. Pretend it doesn't exist and don't even look at the balance. That way you will not be tempted to use it for day-to-day expenses.

The Top Five Benefits of a "What if" Fund

1. Not having to rely on credit cards

2. Decreasing bad debt and your financial burden

3. Having cash available when you need it most

4. Less stress due to knowing you have money to pay for emergencies

5. Having money available for travel, special occasions and lifestyle choices

In the more than 15 years of resolving other people's financial troubles there is little I haven't seen, so it is very important to understand you are not alone, and your situation is not hopeless. Right now you are probably living "paycheck to paycheck" and can't believe there is any way to save money — but there is. It is a question of rethinking priorities and your "what if" fund is a priority.

Life & Debt does work — and it will work for you. It is a step-by-step guide to the light at the end of your financial tunnel and that light includes the ability to have a "safety net" for your "what if" life events.

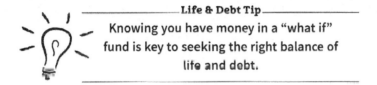

_____ **Life & Debt Tip** _____

Knowing you have money in a "what if" fund is key to seeking the right balance of life and debt.

CHAPTER *19*

Reducing Debt-Related Stress

There are situations in all our lives that are going to be inherently stressful — we simply cannot avoid them and live in the "real world." Money, finances, and bills all are key stressors and you need to avoid the additional stress that comes with deep financial troubles. A classic saying states that money can be "the root of all evil" but it does not have to be, nor is it, negative. However, it needs to be managed properly to be positive.

It is not unusual for clients to tell me during our first meeting about having trouble sleeping, not being able to concentrate, or find themselves always anxious and irritable. Worse, their "bad" debt burden has created a level of stress which now adversely affects nearly every aspect of their lives including health, work and family relationships. Arguing with a partner about money, or being unable to get a decent night's sleep worrying about it, will only create more stress. So, the time to act is now.

Once you use the *Life & Debt* tools outlined in previous chapters to "refocus" and bring your debt down to a manageable level, you will begin to free yourself from debt-related stress and its consequences. To help jump start that process I have organized the following list.

Life & Debt Tips to Reduce Debt-Related Stress

1. Say Goodbye to Credit Cards. I assure you the sky will not fall in if you start using cash or a debit card instead of credit cards. Moving away from credit cards is one of the key steps to financial freedom. They are not for day-to-day needs, or to be used to pay all your expenses — that is what gets you into financial trouble. I am a realist and have one or two credit cards which I use minimally and pay off the balances, as soon as possible, which should be your goal as well. It is all part of *Life & Debt*. See Chapter 17 for more details on breaking the credit card addiction.

2. Use Self-Control while Shopping. Budgeting takes self-control and in Part 2 you learned how easy it can be. Learning to use self-control while shopping can be easy as well. Write up a list before shopping for *anything* and stick to it. Before buying an item that isn't a necessity, take a moment to reflect. Go home and decide if you really want it and then write it into your budget. You could also ask someone in your household who you *know* will only purchase items on your list — and nothing more — to do the household shopping. If there is something you feel you must have, rethink it from the perspective of purchasing it with cash. It will create self-control in deciding whether the item is truly necessary.

3. Avoid "Shopping Therapy." Buying things you don't need when you are emotionally stressed is a quick fix that just leads to more bad debt. Find more constructive and positive outlets to release negative emotions. Be aware of why you are shopping and the thought process behind it. It will help curb your spending.

4. Do Not Keep Up with the Joneses. Having the latest and greatest gear is fine if you are independently wealthy, but since most people are not, societal peer pressure is negative — and unnecessary. It is human nature to make comparisons but finding relief from debt-related stress is your first priority. Refocus your priorities for now, and budgeting for "goodies" as something to look forward to later.

5. Be Honest about Your Entertainment Budget. If your social circle involves big spenders and expensive entertainment venues be honest and assertive about what you can and cannot do right now. People will understand. Suggest less pricy outings or limit the times you go out with the "high rollers." You will be surprised how many people will agree with downsizing entertainment options. Right now you need to lighten up financially so your stress can do the same. You might also find that being honest with people could bring added emotional support, which can only help in achieving your financial goals.

6. Be Kind to Yourself Physically. Stress will tear you down physically if you let it. Make sure you eat right, exercise, get plenty of sleep, and keep your doctor in the loop. You don't need to add a new medical problem to the mix. Some people also find stress relief from meditation. I recommend deep breathing and positive thinking prior to opening any bills. Try doing this before you go to sleep and before you pick up the mail to lessen your anxiety and anticipation. Learn to embrace your bills and create positive energy around paying them so you can break the negative cycle of stress. The bottom line is to take very good care of yourself physically and emotionally during this process.

And remember, you are not alone. You may not know it, but people all around you are struggling with debt as well. Very often people who appear to have no money problems are deeply in debt. I see them in my office all the time.

Life & Debt Tip

Your debt-related stress will lessen as your unmanageable debt becomes more manageable because the two go hand-in-hand.

CHAPTER *20*

Long-Term Goals

Congratulations! With the *Life & Debt* system you have met your short-term financial goals by learning how to embrace your debt and successfully manage it with a working budget and regular monitoring of your credit. You also have started an account for your "what if" fund and made yourself a "payee" on your budget.

Now that you have started the process of turning your "bad" debt into "good" debt, and have it under control, you might be asking yourself, what's next? The answer is: long-term goals. A secure financial future means planning for long-term goals like retirement, a vacation home, or your children's education. Everyone's long-term goals are different. However, if you cannot think of any right now perhaps you want to put away some money in a special fund to use later.

Because you have learned to start saving, you can face the future with a new attitude and eliminate the stress and angst that comes with too much bad debt and the inability to pay it down to manageable levels.

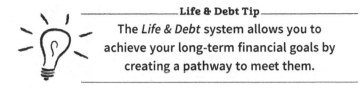

In addition to budgeting and credit monitoring, the *Life & Debt* system emphasizes savings for a good reason — without it you cannot afford to plan for unexpected expenses or future financial goals. In Chapter 18 I discussed in detail why savings and a "what if" fund are important and how to begin. To review, if you have never budgeted for savings, start small and build up to 10% of your net income designated toward a special emergency fund/savings account.

As the account grows, you feel better knowing you have cash on hand so you can make important financial decisions as needed. This means having funds ready in case of an accident or emergency medical or dental work.

EXAMPLES OF LONG-TERM GOALS

Everyone's short term and long term goals are different. Some people just want to be able to pay their bills at the end of the month (with a little left over for savings), while others may plan to travel the world one day. However, there are several long-term goals that many people share, especially parents.

1. Pay Down Your Debt. Throughout *Life & Debt* I have been explaining how important it is to pay down your debt and there is no time like the present. It is the best way to create more cash flow to fund your long-term goals. Make credit cards and loans with high balances your first priority and consider more frequent payments (biweekly instead of monthly) to put a bigger dent in your larger debt balances like mortgages or student loans.

2. Retirement Planning. Just like college expenses, it is never too early, or late, to start thinking about, and planning for, your retirement. Few people could live on their social security checks alone and pensions are rapidly becoming a thing of the past, so I encourage people of all ages to take retirement financial planning seriously. I have had many people tell me they believe they will never have enough money to retire. My advice is to start putting money away now otherwise it may never happen. Open an account and make regular contributions.

There are many different retirement accounts, but many people use the following:

- IRA: This is a personal plan that you contribute to after taxes

- 401(k): A 401(k) is generally an employee incentive program that deducts money from your paycheck. Sometimes your employer will match the funds you designate for deduction.

Before making a decision:

- Check if your employer offers matching or contributing plans
- Find a financial planner you trust

3. Saving for a Home. For most people buying a home is one of the largest investments they will make. It can also be one of the more stressful since it often involves depleting a savings account. A smart way to buy a home is put as much money into the down payment as possible — at least 20% of the purchase price — without emptying your bank account. This long-term goal means you must start saving as soon as possible so you are in a comfortable position when the time is right to buy. Prior to purchasing, save as much as you can, for as long as you can, to keep your future loan payments low.

4. College Education Costs. Every parent wants the best education for their children, but that usually comes with a very expensive price tag if you do not research carefully which school to attend and what you can afford. With the exception of those who are independently wealthy, it is a business decision and a large investment for the majority of parents.

Once you have your debt and finances under control, it is never too early to start a college savings fund. Do a budget so you know what you can afford and what the long-term goal is — the total amount you will need. Also, begin a frank discussion about the cost of higher education with your middle- or high-school-aged children. I have done this with my children. I want them to consider options that make sense financially, as well as for their education.

5. Pay Off Your Student Loans. Whether student loans are yours, or a loan you co-signed for a child, pay them off as quickly as possible. Interest accrues on these loans so the longer you take to pay them off the more money you will spend doing so. Pay the maximum payment each month and make it a priority to put any extra money toward the interest. If you are unable to make the payments, you may be able to ask the loan servicer (check your statement for the institution that manages the loan) for a temporary payment reduction, or to switch to payment plans better suited to your budget — but *always* pay every month.

Paying down loans might mean some hard choices, like returning home to live with your parents for a short period, but it will be worthwhile if you meet the long-term goal of paying the loans off. I have clients who have just finished paying off their own student loans and are now taking out loans for their own children. You do not want to be in this position. There are always options and it is important to know what they are. Study your loans, learn the details of repayment, forbearance, and even default. Though that would not be your intention, things change in life and it is better to be in the know than in the dark.

No matter what your long-term plans are it is comforting to know you will be able to afford them. And the only way to be sure of that is to plan ahead for them.

Life & Debt Tip

Set your long-term goals early in life to be prepared to reach them sooner rather than later.

CHAPTER *21*

Leaving the Paycheck-to-Paycheck Lifestyle Behind

You did it! Now that you have learned how to embrace your debt, start a budget, and monitor your credit and credit scores, you are on the way to financial freedom. The *Life & Debt* system has given you the tools you need to leave the paycheck-to-paycheck lifestyle behind.

People who live paycheck-to-paycheck barely have enough money to pay their bills at the end of the month. They cannot pay down their debt, and there is certainly nothing left for savings or a "what if" fund. This can create negativity about money and paying bills, which can lead to chronic stress and avoiding good financial habits. Once you get a job and start acquiring necessities (like a home) and the bills and lifestyle choices that come with it, you could easily slip into the paycheck-to-paycheck life before you know it. Now that you are using the *Life & Debt* system this will not be your future.

Everything starts with a budget, and now you know how to make one to suit your needs (necessities) and wants (lifestyle choices). You have learned that rethinking your needs and wants can net great rewards — like extra cash for savings and a "what if" fund — all while paying down your debt. Instead of dreading paying your bills, now you can look forward to paying them easily and without stress. I do. I look forward to paying my bills because I have budgeted for them and feel good about paying off my debts. It is a positive experience for me and will be for you as well.

Life & Debt is more than just a financial plan, it is an empowerment plan. It teaches you how to change your perspective on money, income, expenses, and savings from negative to positive. Though being in debt is very stressful, once you embrace your debt and change your thought process from negative to positive you will see the progression in yourself, your finances, and begin to enjoy the benefits that come with it. Realistic budgeting, paying bills on time, paying off your "bad" debt, having a savings account, and the positive reinforcement that comes with financial freedom is now your future. Enjoy it!

FAQs

Are there advantages to having a certain amount of debt?
Yes! Having a manageable amount of debt, which I call "good" debt, allows you to acquire the things you need in life like a home loan. Your debt only becomes "bad" when it is unmanageable (mountains of credit card debt) and you are in a financial crisis because of it. Having debt means someone trusted you enough to extend you credit, and because debt *will* be a part of your life, I advise you get to know it and embrace it.

If I take out a loan to remodel my kitchen, is that "good" debt or "bad" debt?
This depends on the situation. If you do a budget to determine that you can afford a small loan and stay within that budget for a remodeling job, which increases the value of your house to above your loan, it may be good debt. I would only suggest a loan if it can fit within you budget. If you end up struggling to pay back the loan, or you default on it, it will become bad debt.

What is a payday loan and is it "good" debt or "bad" debt?

Bad! Similar to a cash advance, a payday loan is a loan from an independent loan company which usually is the amount of your paycheck. However, it is just like robbing Peter to pay Paul. They are illegal in many states and can come with very high interest rates and fees. Check with your state banking or finance office or attorney general's office first.

Is a car lease a secured debt or unsecured debt?

A car lease is a secured debt, meaning you have a physical item — the car — which can be taken back by the car company. This is known as repossession. An unsecured loan, such as a credit card, is not tied to a physical item.

Which is typically harder to pay off, secured or unsecured debt?

This depends on the amount of the loans, the payments and your priorities. Generally it is harder to pay off secured debts because they tend to be larger, like a home or car. I find that people who rely on credit cards for day-to-day expenses, and who do not have enough money to fully pay their monthly bills, tend to pay their credit card debt (unsecured) first and secured second. Budgeting can help with organizing your priorities and paying all your bills on time.

I was late paying the electric bill a few times. Will this affect my credit?

If you are late paying an electric or utility bill don't panic. Although this is a bad financial habit to adopt, utility companies generally do not report you to the credit bureaus until you are very late, which means more than 30 days. If you do not pay the bill at all it could be sent to a collections agency, which could be reported to the credit bureaus. You might also be sued. Do not let things escalate to these levels. Ask your utility company about balanced billing (paying a set amount each month) which helps your ability to budget.

Do clothes ever fall under discretionary spending?

Absolutely! If you are working to pay off your debt, or saving for a long-term financial goal, discretionary items (things you may want but really don't need) like expensive clothing should wait until you can afford it. Designer jeans may be fashionable today but out of style tomorrow, and you will be no closer to meeting your financial goals. Before purchasing any discretionary item think it through carefully and make sure it makes sense in your budget.

If I am budgeting should I stop eating out several times a week?

Depending on where you do your grocery shopping, it is usually more economical to eat at home, especially if you are feeding a large family. However, going out to dinner occasionally is fun and does not have to be too expensive. Be creative. Check for coupons, two-for-one deals, and venues where children eat free under a certain age.

How do you determine how much to designate for retirement savings, "what if" funds, and college savings?

This depends on your income and budget. I always suggest starting with 10% of your net income, which is the amount prior to taxes being taken out. Find out what kind of retirement plans are offered by your employer and see if there are matching plans — meaning your employer will match the amount you designate for a retirement fund. Also, never borrow from your retirement account — that is what your separate "what if" fund is for. You can discuss retirement plans and saving for college expenses with a financial planner. Do your research and choose a planner you feel can be the most helpful with meeting your short-term and long-term financial goals.

What is the main reason why people avoid setting up a budget?
People avoid budgeting for all sorts of reasons including fear, boredom, or an aversion to math. Many avoid it because they think it is tedious, and some believe it is frightening to see where their money is being spent and how much debt they have. Though I understand all of this, I can assure you budgeting is not scary and much easier than you think. It is an essential part of removing your debt as discussed throughout this book and *you can do it!* Some people also think budgeting takes too much time, but today there are many programs and technology options to make budgeting quick and easy.

What are some good budgeting tips for someone on a variable (non-fixed) income?
Make a list of your expenses and divide them into fixed (the amount is always the same) and variable (the amount can fluctuate). Try to anticipate how much the variable expenses will increase. This way you can pay your bills today and be ready when things change. I suggest you make a monthly budget based on the least amount you can expect to earn that month. Working with a lower number will leave you with a surplus and help prepare for times when the money may be tight.

How often should I get a copy of my credit report?
The minimum is once a year from all three credit bureaus — TransUnion, Equifax, Experian. However if you are trying to improve your overall credit standing consider subscribing to a credit monitoring service that will send you quarterly reports with your credit report and score. These companies will also alert you whenever something changes on your credit report. Study your reports so you can understand how your score is calculated and what you can do to improve it. To help prevent fraud, always make sure any activity on the report is accurate and approved by you.

Do credit scores typically fluctuate a lot?

Absolutely. Your credit score can change in a blink of an eye! If you keep good financial habits and pay your bills on time you will see positive results such as a higher score. On the other hand, if you miss a payment on one of your debts for more than30 days or more, you may see your score drop. Learn what factors determine why your score goes up and down.

What are some warning signs that a debt resolution organization or person isn't reputable?

I advise you to avoid organizations asking for fees upfront who do not have a local office where you can meet in person. Also check with your state attorney general's office and bank or financial department to see if they are licensed in your state. Search reputable online sites for information about the organization.

What are some of the ways to recover my credit after a bankruptcy?

Try to accrue as little debt as possible. Resist applying for too much new credit and begin with just a few small accounts. Only charge what you can pay in full at the end of the month. If you have less revolving debt, meaning credit you do not pay off completely which then revolves to the next month with interest, it is less likely you will become overextended again. Monitor your credit reports and move to a more cash-based budget to avoid the need for credit. With time, patience, and careful financial planning, your credit can recover.

Are 20 credit cards too many?

Yes! Few people can manage the kind of debt that comes with a wallet full of credit cards, and no one needs 20. That is recipe for financial disaster. You really only need a few credit cards — and they should be held in reserve. To lessen your overall debt and take back control of your finances your primary payment method needs to be a debit card or cash. However, the first step to breaking a credit card addiction is to "just say no" to your existing cards and any new offers.

Are retail store cards a good deal because of all the discounts and rewards they offer?

No! The higher interest rates on retail credit cards (as opposed to bank credit cards) are not worth the savings you receive in store discounts unless you pay the bill in full each month. Otherwise those higher interest rates will quickly eat up your discounts and rewards. If you have an interest-free card make sure you pay off the balance before the interest-free period expires.

Can debit cards or cash be substituted for credit cards?

Yes. Today you can use a debit card or prepaid credit card almost everywhere a credit card is accepted. Some of my clients worry about not be able to get a hotel room, or rent a car, without an actual credit card, but this is not usually the case. Fortunately there are alternatives.

Is medical debt handled differently than other kinds of debt?

Typically medical debt is resolvable but handled differently than other types of debt. Also, setting up a payment plan with a provider can be easier. I suggest you do not delay since medical debt can be sent to a collection agency and reported on your credit report. Try to work with the hospital or service provider to agree on a payment plan before this happens.

APPENDIX II

Sample Credit Report

Regular monitoring of your credit report is part of the *Life & Debt* system of smart money management. Following is a sample online credit report courtesy of Experian, one of the three major credit bureaus in the United States.*

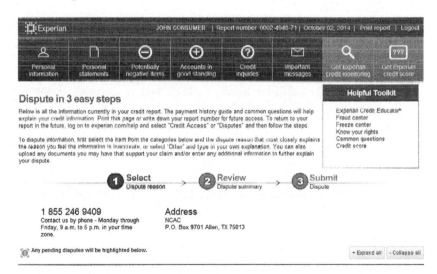

*Credit report language and content are subject to change.

Personal information

Name(s) associated with your credit

Name	Name identification number	
JON CONSUMER	9466	Dispute
J CONSUMER	14218	Dispute

Address(es) associated with your credit

Address	Address identification number	Residence type	Geographical code	
1234 ELM ST PORTLAND OR 97209-3482	0575721840	Apartment complex	0-500000-51-6440	Dispute
123 FIRST ST PORTLAND OR 97209-2868	0570556850	Apartment complex	0-500000-51-6440	Dispute

Other personal information associated with your credit

Year of birth

1955	Dispute

Spouse or co-applicant

MARY	Dispute

Telephone number(s)

260 555 1234	Dispute
800 555 1234	Dispute
306 555 1234	Dispute

Current or former employer(s)	Address	
XYZ CORPORATION	123 MAIN, ANYTOWN, NY 11105	Dispute
ABC INC.	55 MAIN BLVD. ANYTOWN, NY 11105	Dispute

back to top

Your personal statements

No general personal statements appear on your report.

Add personal statement

back to top

Potentially negative items

No **Public record** items appear on your report.

	Account name	Account number	Recent balance	Date opened	Status	
+	123 MORTGAGE SERVICES	874005660...	$66,671 as of 08/01/2011	11/2009	Open.	Dispute
+	ABC LOAN SVCS	8417001750....	$13,347 as of 08/17/2011	11/2007	Open.	Dispute
+	XYZ HOME LOANS	21...	$128,181 as of 07/28/2011	06/2008	Open.	Dispute

back to top

Accounts in good standing

	Account name	Account number	Recent balance	Date opened	Status	
+	MYTOWN CREDIT	014057512013348892	Not reported	01/1989	Paid/Never late.	Dispute
+	BANK OF MYTOWN	4407441999202...	Not reported	07/2005	Paid/Never late.	Dispute
+	LOANS R US	442710004087....	$5,129 as of 08/08/2011	02/2010	Open/Never late.	Dispute
+	EZ LOANS	539870001000....	$15,110 as of 08/27/2011	04/1998	Open/Never late.	Dispute

back to top

Credit inquiries

We make your credit history available to your current and prospective creditors and employers as allowed by law. Personal data about you may be made available to companies whose products and services may interest you. As required by the Fair Credit Reporting Act, we display these requests for your credit history as a record of fact.

Inquiries shared with others ⑦

Account name	Date of request	
⊕ EZ LOANS	12/20/2010	Options
⊕ MY CREDIT SVCS	09/28/2009	Options
⊕ MY CREDIT SVCS	09/14/2009	Options

Inquiries shared only with you ⑦

Account name	Date of request(s)	
⊕ MY MOTOR CREDIT	08/02/2011	Options
⊕ ABCD FIN SVCS	06/18/2011	Options
⊕ MYTOWN FINANCIAL	08/09/2009	Options

back to top

Important messages

Experian collects and organizes information about you and your credit history from public records, your creditors and other reliable sources. By law, we cannot disclose certain behavioral information (relating to physical, mental, or behavioral health or condition). Although we do not generally collect such information, it could appear in the name of a data furnisher (i.e., "Cancer Center") that reports your payment history to us. If so, those names display in your report, but in reports to others they display only as "Medical Information Provider." Consumer statements included on your report at your request that contain medical information are disclosed to others.

back to top

Know your rights

Para informacion en espanol, visite www.consumerfinance.gov/learnmore o escribe a la Consumer Financial Protection Bureau, 1700 G Street N.W., Washington, D.C. 20552.

A Summary of Your Rights under the Fair Credit Reporting Act

The federal Fair Credit Reporting Act (FCRA) promotes the accuracy, fairness, and privacy of information in the files of consumer reporting agencies. There are many types of consumer reporting agencies, including credit bureaus and specialty agencies (such as agencies that sell information about check writing histories, medical records, and rental history records). Here is a summary of your major rights under the FCRA. For more information, including information about additional rights, go to www.consumerfinance.gov/learnmore or write to: Consumer Financial Protection Bureau, 1700 G Street N.W., Washington, D.C. 20552.

You must be told if information in your file has been used against you. Anyone who uses a credit report or another type of consumer report to deny your application for credit, insurance, or employment or to take another adverse action against you must tell you, and must give you the name, address, and phone number of the agency that provided the information.

You have the right to know what is in your file. You may request and obtain all the information about you in the files of a consumer reporting agency (your "file disclosure"). You will be required to provide proper identification, which may include your Social Security number. In many cases, the disclosure will be free. You are entitled to a free file disclosure if:

a person has taken adverse action against you because of information in your credit report;

you are the victim of identify theft and place a fraud alert in your file;

your file contains inaccurate information as a result of fraud;

you are on public assistance;

you are unemployed but expect to apply for employment within 60 days.

All consumers are entitled to one free disclosure every 12 months upon request from each nationwide credit bureau and from nationwide specialty consumer reporting agencies. See www.consumerfinance.gov/learnmore for additional information.

You have the right to ask for a credit score. Credit scores are numerical summaries of your credit-worthiness based on information from credit bureaus. You may request a credit score from consumer reporting agencies that create scores or distribute scores used in residential real property loans, but you will have to pay for it. In some mortgage transactions, you will receive credit score information for free from the mortgage lender.

You have the right to dispute incomplete or inaccurate information. If you identify information in your file that is incomplete or inaccurate, and report it to the consumer reporting agency, the agency must investigate unless your dispute is frivolous. See www.consumerfinance.gov/learnmore for an explanation of dispute procedures.

Consumer reporting agencies must correct or delete inaccurate, incomplete, or unverifiable information. Inaccurate, incomplete or unverifiable information must be removed or corrected, usually within 30 days. However, a consumer reporting agency may continue to report information it has verified as accurate.

Consumer reporting agencies may not report outdated negative information. In most cases, a consumer reporting agency may not report negative information that is more than seven years old, or bankruptcies that are more than 10 years old.

Paper versions of your credit report may vary but should contain the following basic information categories:

1. Personal Information. Your name and report number is listed at the very top of the Experian document. Keep the report number handy for easy reference. Experian also lists its contact information and steps to follow if you want to dispute inaccuracies found in the report.

The report will then list your name, any aliases (also known as) — that could include a married or maiden name — past and present addresses, past and present employers, your spouse, or co-applicant, and telephone numbers. It also has a name identification number, which is how Experian identifies the names associated with respective accounts. You will also see a geographical code that Experian uses to identify each address according to state, county, census tract, and block group.

2. Personal Statements. Though there are no personal statements in this sample, any disputes about inaccuracies you register will be listed within that section of the report.

3. Potentially Negative Items. This section contains a listing of anything a creditor may view as negative such as late payments, bankruptcies, judgments, or liens. Public records will appear first. Though this sample report does not have any listed, public records accounts are associated with a legal action such as a bankruptcy, foreclosure, property lien or a judgment from the court or tax liens. See Chapter 11 for more information on these types of accounts.

Below the public records section will be a list of negative credit activity reported to Experian. Negative credit activity might include missed payments or a default. See Chapter 10 for more detail.

4. Accounts in Good Standing. These accounts are currently open, meaning they are being used by you, and in "good standing" because you are making regular payments of the required amount of money set by the creditor. You may not have available credit on these accounts but they are not delinquent, which is a good thing for your credit.

5. Credit Inquiries. There are two types of inquiries on this report — "Inquiries Shared With Others" and "Inquiries Shared Only by You."

> **Inquiries Shared with Others** lists requests initiated by you, like applying for a car loan, which is considered a *hard inquiry (pg. 96)*. In brief you are giving the bank or lender permission to check your credit and this listing will include general information about that creditor.

> **Inquiries Shared Only by You** refers to creditors who viewed your credit information without your permission. These are considered *soft inquiries (pg. 96)* meaning they do not affect your credit eligibility. They might include potential creditors screening you for pre-approved credit card offers or existing creditors viewing your report.

This completes the personal part of your report. The report closes with legal disclaimers regarding medical information and a summary of your rights under the Fair Credit Reporting Act. It is a good idea to know your rights as a consumer particularly in the age of identity theft.

ACKNOWLEDGEMENTS

I wish to personally thank the following people for their contributions, assistance, and support. For without them, this book could not have come to fruition.

First of all, I especially want to extend my thanks to Vicki DiStefano for being my right hand during the entire project. She has been there for me every step of the way, and her sage counsel and positive encouragement kept me focused, on track, and helped to make this book a reality.

Secondly, I wish to thank Karen Jones for all of her editorial expertise and guidance, as well as Meryl Moss Media Relations and her team who provided expert advice as well as strategic and tactical thinking from the beginning of this process to the end, making my vision possible.

Last, but not least, all of this could not be imaginable without the love and support of my children, and for this I am truly grateful.

LESLIE TAYNE, ESQ., is a highly respected consumer and business debt-related attorney and advisor. Tayne founded Tayne Law Group, P.C., which is one of the few in New York State concentrating solely in debt resolution solutions and alternatives to filing bankruptcy for consumers, small business owners, and professionals. Recognized as an industry leader, her achievements include being selected for the Long Island Business News' Leadership in Law Awards, twice honored as one of Long Island Business News' Top 50 Most Influential Women in Business, and presented with the Achievers' Award at Long Island Center for Business & Professional Women. As a private citizen and volunteer, she is actively involved with the Guide Dog Foundation for the Blind, Inc., Smithtown, NY., caring for and training puppies who eventually become service dogs for individuals in need.

CPSIA information can be obtained at www.ICGtesting.com
Printed in the USA
BVOW06s1720311215

431434BV00021B/688/P

9 780986 349508